Praise for
WHAT LOVE IS

"Anyone feeling disenchanted or discomforted by the itchy constraints
of traditional, heteronormative, monogamous, pair-bonded, procreative,
romantic love will be well-served to read Jenkins' accessible and incisive
treatise on what love is. Within her argumentation is a well-placed critique of the misogyny and heterosexism woven throughout traditional
philosophical and scientific discourse on love. Through a feminist lens,
she studies these biases and reveals their links to contemporary beliefs
about love and relationships, highlighting how these constructs ultimately constrain expressions of affection from the many possible configurations that, for some, may be more satisfying than the monolithic
norm of monogamous, heterosexual love. Hers is a readable, entertain-
ing, and poignant commentary on the current state of thinking, sure to
ignite passionate conversation while working to dissolve the artificial
boundaries limiting our experience of love."

—Meredith L. Chivers, Associate Professor
of Psychology, Queen's University

What Love Is

What Love Is

and what it could be

Carrie Jenkins

BASIC BOOKS
New York

Copyright © 2017 by Caroline Susanne Jenkins

Published in the United States
by Basic Books
an imprint of Perseus Books, LLC,
a subsidiary of Hachette Book Group, Inc.

All rights reserved. Printed in the United States of America. No part of this
book may be reproduced in any manner whatsoever without written
permission except in the case of brief quotations embodied in
critical articles and reviews. For information, address
Basic Books
250 West 57th Street, 15th floor
New York, NY 10107.

Books published by Basic Books are available at special discounts for bulk
purchases in the United States by corporations, institutions, and other
organizations. For more information, please contact the
Special Markets Department at Perseus Books
2300 Chestnut Street, Suite 200, Philadelphia, PA 19103
or call (800) 810-4145, ext. 5000
or e-mail special.markets@perseusbooks.com.

Designed by Amy Quinn

Library of Congress Cataloging-in-Publication Data

Names: Jenkins, Carrie, author.
Title: What love is : and what it could be / Carrie Jenkins.
Description: New York : Basic Books [2017]
Includes bibliographical references and index.

Identifiers:
LCCN 2016019598| ISBN 9780465098859 (HC) | ISBN 9780465098866 (EB)

Subjects: LCSH: Love--Philosophy.
Classification: LCC BD436 .J46 2017 | DDC 128/.46--dc23 LC record available at
https://lccn.loc.gov/2016019598

10 9 8 7 6 5 4 3 2 1

For philosophy with love.
P.S. We need to talk.

Contents

Prologue   On Being a Philosopher in Love (Maybe)   ix

             Introduction   1

Chapter 1   Love Is Biology   17

Chapter 2   Love Is Society   37

Chapter 3   Gems at the Garage Sale:
             Philosophers on Love   55

Chapter 4   Love Is as Love Does: Love's Dual Nature   79

Chapter 5   Under Construction: Love's Changing Role   105

Chapter 6   What Needs to Change   123

Chapter 7   It's Love, Jim, but Not as We Know It:
             The Future (via the Past)   147

Coda   Make It So   167

             Acknowledgments   183

             Notes   185

             Index   199

Prologue:
On Being a Philosopher in Love (Maybe)

I am a philosopher. I am also a human being. These aren't wholly separable aspects of my self—they are intimately connected. They inform and shape each other. How I love influences how I think, and how I think influences how I love. I'm not unusual in this regard. Anyone who sets out to think about love comes to the task with a bundle of personal experiences. Whether good or bad, stereotypical or subversive, our experiences inform our thinking. And there is nothing wrong with that—which is lucky, really, as there's certainly no escaping it! We just need to be aware that it happens.

On the mornings when I walk from my boyfriend's apartment to the home I share with my husband, I sometimes find myself reflecting on the disconnects between my own experiences with romantic love and the way romantic love is normally understood in the time and place in which I live (Vancouver, Canada, in 2016). Sometimes this starts out in my mind as a replay of an awkward conversation, one of those where someone's asked me a perfectly innocent question—"So how do you two know each other?"—and unwittingly forced me to choose between giving a deceptive answer and providing what I know will be *too much information.*

If I tell the truth—"He's my boyfriend"—to people who know me and my husband, it's inevitably going to cause embarrassment—the kind of embarrassment that comes with suddenly being made to acknowledge the existence of something awkward, something abnormal, something that makes people feel icky. Deceptive answers—"Oh, he used to work in the office upstairs from mine"—are easy and comfortable.

And it turns out, it's alarmingly easy to be dishonest while saying true things. He really did work in the office upstairs from mine; that just isn't how we met. In fact we never met in person until we noticed each other on the dating website OKCupid. When I am tired or nervous, when I don't know the person I'm talking to very well, or when I just don't feel like explaining myself again, I take the easy way out. I give the deceptive answer.

But philosophy doesn't let me take the easy way out of hard questions. Living in this cultural context, I'm routinely reminded that successful, mature, romantic love—the stuff of movies, pop songs, Valentine's Day cards, and fairy tales—is supposed to be monogamous. So the question is forced on me: What is this thing that I'm doing? Is it love? Is it *romantic* love?

Philosophy is my day job, and I know a philosophical question when I see one. But reading the philosophical literature on love hasn't, on the whole, been much help to me. Philosophers often assume monogamy without question. Some even treat monogamy as definitive of romantic love: a characterizing feature that distinguishes it from other kinds of love.[1] No doubt these philosophers are guided by their own experiences, which create and sustain their baseline assumptions. But philosophy no more allows our baseline assumptions to pass unchallenged than it lets us take the easy way out of hard questions.

If indeed romantic love must be monogamous, then I am making some kind of mistake when I say, "I'm in love with you"—meaning romantically—to both my partners. I am not lying, because I am genuinely trying to be as honest as I can. But if romantic love requires monogamy, then despite my best intentions, what I'm saying at those moments is not, strictly speaking, true.

The question of whether what I say is true is complicated, not least because the nature of love is a vague and messy business. Answers are not going to appear neatly tied up with a heart-shaped bow. We can and should trace out the broad-brush contours of love, but if we go looking for sharp edges—a tidy, simple theory—we are bound to be disappointed. Trying to state the nature of romantic love with precision is like trying to nail some Jell-O to a wall made of Jell-O, using a Jell-O nail.

But the question is complicated for another reason as well. Romantic love is in the process of changing. And I don't just mean that attitudes toward love are changing, although that's also true. I'll unpack these ideas over the course of the book. For now, though, suffice it to say that I think the norm of monogamy could be one of the features in flux. We are creating space in our ongoing cultural conversations to question the universal norm of monogamous love, just as we previously created space to question the universal norm of hetero love.

Just having the words to describe something is an important first step in opening up that space. A word for honest, nonmonogamous, loving relationships, "polyamory," came into circulation during the late twentieth century. Since the 1990s, the Internet has also greatly facilitated the exploration of polyamory and other forms of ethical nonmonogamy (as distinct from cheating and other unethical behaviors). This has made it infinitely easier for those who wanted to explore nonmonogamy to find like-minded partners, communities, and information. Over the same period, researchers have begun to work on understanding the stigma attached to violations of the monogamy norm, while activists and advocates have begun to work on ending that stigma and providing practical information and support to people whose families or jobs are at risk because of prejudice surrounding their nonmonogamous relationships.

One can track the effects of all this in various cultural barometers. Dan Savage, one of the world's most famous (and controversial) sex and relationship advice columnists, is one such barometer. Over the last few years, Savage has started to take the possibility of mature, successful nonmonogamous romantic love very seriously, having previously been something of a doubting Thomas on the question of whether people in poly "marriages" ever made it to their third anniversary.[2] Themes and questions related to modern polyamory have also started to appear at the more thoughtful end of mass media. In the Spike Jonze movie *Her*, for instance, a computer operating system claims to be in love with 641 people. She attempts to explain to one human lover that "the heart's not like a box that gets filled up. It expands in size the more you love."

It's too early to say where this conversation will go. I think romantic love might expand to include nonmonogamous love as part of a general trend toward greater inclusion. It's not that a norm of nonmonogamy would replace the norm of monogamy (any more than a norm of nonheterosexuality is replacing the norm of heterosexuality). Rather, the scope of what counts as romantic love would become more inclusive. But I don't see this future as a done deal. It's not even as close to being a done deal as the inclusion of nonhetero love. And all this means that I am unsure whether nonmonogamous love is really *romantic* love—whether being "in love" in that sense with two people is really possible, here and now.

I think love can make room for nonmonogamy. But, of course, I am biased. (Then again, everyone is biased.) Perhaps it would be safer to say that I hope love can make room for non-monogamy. A more inclusive picture of love would make better sense of what's happened in my own life than the image I grew up with, which made romantic love the property of straight monogamous couples only.

In any case, I am prepared to bet that, from a biological perspective, what's happening in my brain looks the way romantic love is supposed to look. In fact, it's partly for that reason that I think romantic love could accommodate nonmonogamous love. Romantic love has a long history of breaking free from social constraints, and biology has played a part in that. But the interplay between love's constraints and its freedoms is complicated, as is the interplay between love's biology and its social profile.

On those mornings walking home, I came to realize that in order to understand whether I was in love or not, I'd have to work on untangling some of these complications. I couldn't think of a better approach to the problem than to search for an answer to the philosophical question, What is romantic love? (This is what I meant when I said philosophy doesn't let me take the easy way out!) My efforts developed into this book. But the project quickly outgrew its original purpose of helping me figure out whether I was "in love." It has ended up being all kinds of other things I never anticipated. This isn't a book about nonmonogamy per se— although it sprang partly from questions I have about that. Love turns out to be philosophically fascinating for all kinds of reasons I could never have imagined. This is a short book, but even so, it'll take us into the realms of medicine, magic, queerness, wisdom, dopamine, gender, Romans, rainbows, rationality, Sappho, soul mates, politics, and, of course, human nature. Buckle up!

Eventually this book became an exploration of possibility: what love could be, not just what it is. I ended up with a theory that makes romantic love partly (but not entirely) a social construct. The social aspect of romantic love changes over time, but social change is often slow, especially when it comes to something so invested with value and significance as love. Change doesn't happen overnight, and a single individual can't bring it about. That said, some changes happen quickly enough to be visible in the course of a lifetime, and we do live in interesting times in this regard.

I often wonder what it would take for one particular change—the inclusion of nonmonogamous love as "normal"—to happen. It would have to become unsurprising to see a romantic comedy that ends with a happy romantic relationship among three people or to hear a pop song about the trials of navigating simultaneous open relationships. In other words, becoming included is a numbers game. Exposure to just one example of successful nonmonogamous love may be enough to challenge prejudices.* But it would take exposure to many and varied examples for nonmonogamous love to start to become an acknowledged "normal" option. I don't see this happening anytime soon, although I would be happy to be proved wrong.

In this book you will find my theory of what love is and what it could be. It's a theory that explains why representation in mass media is so important to "nontraditional" love and why we encounter such visceral resistance from the people who want to keep it off our screens and out of the minds of "the children." The crux of the matter is that the representation of romantic love in our cultural products is no mere shadow, or reflection, of what love is. What we see on our screens, hear on our radios, and read in our magazines is actually part of the process of constructing love: making love what it is. These acts of representation are part of how we collectively create and sustain the contours of romantic love's social profile.

The stakes are high. And I'm personally invested, as are you. Just as we all bring our experiences with us, and just as we are all biased, we are all personally invested. Nobody is agenda-free, and there's no "view from nowhere" when it comes to love. It's just that when your "view from somewhere" isn't one of the "normal" ones, you are forcibly and frequently reminded of its existence.

For a philosopher, these reminders of one's own perspective are invaluable (which is not to say they're always nice). Calling ourselves objective doesn't make us any less biased (in fact, there is some evidence that it may make us more so).[3] Being "normal"

---

* This is one reason why "coming out" is important, if and when it's safe to do so.

doesn't mean you have no perspective and no baggage, although it does mean you're less likely to notice these things. In any case, we can't make genuine philosophical progress on the hard questions by stuffing our personal baggage behind the sofa of "objectivity" and hoping nobody looks there. The best we can do is to try to maximize our awareness of whatever it is we're bringing along for the ride.

Introduction

This sense of wonder is the mark of the philosopher. Philosophy indeed has no other origin, and he was a good genealogist who made Iris the daughter of Thaumas.

—Plato, *Theaetetus*[1]

My day job as a philosophy professor consists of thinking, writing, and talking about, as well as teaching, philosophy. I have been a professional philosopher for ten years; before that, I studied philosophy for seven years. Those seventeen years comprise my entire adult life. But as is the case for many people, my childhood was full of philosophy too; I just didn't know it was called "philosophy" back then. Like a lot of kids (until adults tell them to cut it out) I asked questions about the nature of reality as soon as I could entertain them. I wanted to know what existed, what the world was like, and what was possible.

When we wonder what love is, that's part of the philosophical enterprise. More specifically, it's part of metaphysics: the ongoing

1

project of trying to figure out what is real, what the world is like, and what is possible. There is more philosophy going on in people's everyday lives than you might think. Is love real? What is it like? What is possible in the realm of love? These are deep—and old—metaphysical questions. And for a few years now, I've been captivated by them. I never planned to work on love; I started my career thinking about the philosophy of mathematics. But love snuck up on me and wouldn't let me drop it. The mind wants what it wants.

I'm particularly fascinated by romantic love. That's not because I think other kinds of love aren't interesting or important— they certainly are. But our current state of information has landed us with particular philosophical challenges and puzzles when it comes to understanding the nature of romantic love. These puzzles hit me in the heart first, but they quickly took root in my intellectual life as well, connecting themselves in fascinating ways to the other philosophical questions I work on. This part shouldn't have come as a surprise. Philosophically, it's always been my experience that everything is connected to everything else. (That's part of why I love philosophy: a discipline where nothing is, in principle, irrelevant.) As my thinking about love gradually drew in ideas from other areas of philosophy, I was delighted to find they seemed to be just what I needed to make better sense of love.

While the nature of romantic love is a perennial philosophical question, today we are confronting new and immediate pressures to find answers. But doing so can appear less feasible than ever because we also face some especially difficult choices right now. In particular, we face a stark choice between treating romantic love as a biological phenomenon and viewing it as a social or cultural product.

Wikipedia can be a surprisingly good gauge of situations like this. To some extent, it tracks the pulse of our current state of public information. As of this writing,[2] the Wikipedia entry for "love" describes exactly the choice I have in mind: "Biological models of love tend to see it as a mammalian drive, similar to hunger or thirst. Psychology sees love as more of a social and cultural phenomenon. Certainly love is influenced by hormones . . . and how people think and behave in love is influenced by their conceptions of love."

This is actually a great summary of the problem. Some leading theories of love tell us it's a biological phenomenon, while other leading theories (here attributed to psychology but also coming to us from a number of other disciplines) tell us it's a social and cultural phenomenon. There seems to be at least a grain—and perhaps much more than a grain—of truth in both pictures. I believe we can build a philosophical theory that accommodates both the biological and social natures of romantic love. It just takes some conceptual work to see how it all fits together. But the intellectual, practical, and personal payoffs are worth the effort.

Many philosophers of love treat it as a psychological or mental phenomenon, often as an emotion of some kind. I don't think this is the whole story, as we'll see. In any case, the philosophical problems that strike me as most urgent right now have to do with untangling love's biological and social aspects. So while I'm not setting the psychology of love aside—it will keep popping up throughout the book—I've set my sights on questions that point both within and beyond psychology.

If the history of popular culture in the last half century is anything to go by, questions about the nature of romantic love are very important. Several pop songs and albums have "What Is Love?" as their exact titles; Haddaway's 1993 power ballad is perhaps the best known (and my favorite). Then there are variants like the Foreigner song "I Want to Know What Love Is" and the Cole Porter show number "What Is This Thing Called Love?" There are many, many more in the same vein. When a theme is this pronounced in popular culture, that tells us something: we are seriously fascinated and confused by this thing called "love."

It's worth pausing here to notice how often, in these songs and everywhere else, people say "love" when they mean *romantic love*. That's convenient shorthand—but notice how it also suggests romantic love is accorded a special place in our thinking. Anyhow, I'll use it myself: unless I specify otherwise, you can assume that "love" means romantic love throughout this book.

While this fascination with figuring love out is completely contemporary, it is anything but new. The ancient Greek philosopher Plato was obsessed with love of all kinds, not least the kind he called *eros* ("passionate love" or "desire"), which he thought of as something that normally occurred between an older man and a younger man. In Plato's famous *Symposium*, the character Aristophanes expounds a myth about soul mates that sounds like it might be an early theory of romantic love. The story goes that once upon a time humans were a species of two-headed, eight-limbed creatures. But they attracted the wrath of the gods, and so to punish them Zeus split each creature in half. Some split into one woman and one man; others split into either two women or two men. The nature of love, according to this myth, is a striving to reunite with the person who is literally one's "other half."

A much more modern storyteller, contemporary writer Simon Rich, says that the Aristophanes myth leaves out "the vast majority of humans." In his very short story "The Children of the Dirt,"[3] Rich calls the woman-woman pairs "children of the earth," the man-man pairs "children of the sun," and the mixed pairs "children of the moon." But he goes on to say that there were also the "children of the dirt," who only ever had one head and four limbs. They did not get split in half, because Zeus decided they were in enough trouble already. Today, Rich writes, "the vast majority of humans are descendants of the children of the dirt. And no matter how long they search the earth, they'll never find what they're looking for because there's nobody for them, not anybody in the world."

It's true that the Aristophanes myth ignores a lot of single people (both miserable and contented ones). In another respect, though, it is striking to modern ears how inclusive the myth is: the idea of a single creature splitting into two women, two men, or one of each is an attempt to theorize same-sex love right alongside opposite-sex love. We are only just catching up with the 2,000-year-old methodological insight that this might be a good idea.

The myth of soul mates still makes for a great story, with or without Rich's modern addition. But nowadays we don't give it much weight as a realistic explanation of what love is. These days, instead of turning to myths and legends, we look to our own modern oracle: Google. And Google, in turn, looks back, watching what we ask for, tracking levels of public interest in "What is . . ." questions. Unsurprisingly, "What is love?" is constantly at or near the top of the list.[4]

This search for understanding is not simply a quest for intellectual satisfaction, like solving a crossword. Not knowing what love is makes us deeply vulnerable, because love matters: many people make their most significant life choices on the basis of whether they're in love (or think they are). Saying "I love you" is a big deal, and it is worth making every effort to figure out what it means. We can't afford to risk talking past one another or being badly misunderstood in some of the most important conversations of our lives.

And yet people routinely do take that kind of risk; they say "I love you" without thinking—or talking—about what it means to say those words. In some of the worst-case scenarios, as bell hooks has warned in her book *All About Love*, unclarity about the nature of love can lead to mistaking abuse for love.[5] Other people get through life—and love—just fine without thinking much about what love is. But a little reflection would take some of the luck and risk out of this situation.

And what does it say about modern life that so many people's biggest decisions are based on the imagined presence or absence of something so poorly understood as romantic love? It means we have normalized two halves of a situation that, when we stop to think about it, should not strike us as normal. On the one hand, we've accepted the idea of love as a tremendously significant social force: something that shapes and reshapes the entire trajectories of lives and serves as a focal point for all kinds of values. Many of our most strongly held personal, ethical, and political beliefs cluster around our attitudes toward romantic love. (Think about it: you can learn an awful lot about someone's worldview by learning what kinds of love strike that person as normal, natural, or valuable.)

On the other hand, we have simultaneously normalized the idea that love is a mystery: something hard or impossible to comprehend. We as a society cannot agree even on the fundamentals of what love is. In fact, we sometimes revel in or glorify this very lack of understanding, as if incomprehensibility were actually part of what is special or valuable about love. I call this phenomenon the "romantic mystique."

The idea of a "romantic mystique" takes inspiration from an older idea. In 1963, Betty Friedan noticed that people were simultaneously mystifying and glorifying femininity; she called this the "feminine mystique," the idea that femininity is "so mysterious and intuitive and close to the creation and origin of life that man-made science may never be able to understand it." Femininity so conceived is supposedly "special" and "different" from masculinity but not inferior. According to the feminine mystique, "the root of women's troubles in the past is that women envied men, women tried to be like men, instead of accepting their own nature, which can find fulfillment only in sexual passivity, male domination, and nurturing maternal love."[6]

The romantic mystique, as I see it, has a lot in common with the feminine mystique. The romantic mystique tells us that romantic love is also "mysterious and intuitive and close to the creation and origin of life," yet special and wonderful (partly for that very reason). The romantic mystique likewise encourages us to accept love's "nature," passively and uncomprehendingly,

instead of trying to resist or alter it. It is a disempowering ideology that celebrates ignorance and acquiescence.

With love and with women, there is cultural potency to the
idea that mysteriousness is part of what is special about them.
And the connection is no accident: there is a deeply embedded
perception that romantic love falls within the sphere of wom-
en's concerns. (Think about the gender balance among readers
of romance novels, or what we count as a "chick flick," or which
gender is associated with all the pink and fluffy fripperies of
Valentine's Day paraphernalia.) It's no coincidence that love and
women have been placed on the same side of the mysterious-
versus-comprehensible divide.

And it's probably not a coincidence that some of the most
powerful contemporary work on what love really is—and why an-
swering that question matters so much—comes from a feminist
author who also works on gender, bell hooks. hooks is interested
in all kinds of love, but love within romantic relationships is
prominent among her concerns. She thinks we need a definition
of love (particularly one that clarifies that love is incompatible
with abuse), because lacking a definition we run a serious risk
of mistaking abusive situations for loving ones. I'm not sure it's
exactly a definition that we need, but the gist of this thinking
resonates with me. To acquiesce or even revel in our own lack
of understanding of love is not just intellectually unsatisfying; it
exposes us to risk. It means refusing to arm ourselves with the
knowledge and skills we need to stay safe and make good decisions. It means we are failing to understand a lot of what goes on
around us day to day and are paying the price for that—whatever
that price may be.

When something is dangerous but insidious, just identifying and labeling it can be half the battle. That's why I want to start some conversations in which we can discuss the romantic mystique by name. Treating love as massively important yet totally incomprehensible shouldn't strike us as normal. It is a disaster: we are basing some of the key decisions of our lives on something we treat as an inexplicable mystery. Why aren't we more worried about this?

One thing that I suspect is propping up the romantic mystique is a fear that overthinking it will have negative consequences for our own love lives. Perhaps we fear that understanding love too thoroughly might make us bad at loving. Perhaps we worry that we'll lose faith and become cynical about love if we think too hard about it. Because many hold love to be extremely valuable, anxiety about losing it or screwing it up by overthinking it will be a powerful motivator not to do too much thinking. But things that motivate us not to think are dangerous.

John Shand, who teaches philosophy at the Open University in the United Kingdom, has argued that because our everyday ways of thinking about love are contradictory, we risk "destroying the love that we value by the mere act of applied analysis."[7] He tells a cautionary tale about the dangers of overthinking it: "Look at it too closely, and thereby reveal the paradoxes involved in love, and love fails to work its magic. Many loving relationships, I suggest, involve a suspension of disbelief, useful fictions. . . . [D]o not think about it too hard, do not take it apart to see what is really going on, and one will find that it works."

This, I suppose, must be true to Shand's experience. Yet he says that his theory "is derived significantly from the phenomenology of love as encountered in our lives," where the first person plural suggests that Shand thinks his experience is shared. But my experience is not like this at all. I have not found that thinking carefully and philosophically about love has caused it to evaporate. On the contrary, it's made me feel safer and more confident, aware, secure, and genuine in my own relationships. It's also made love—and life—more interesting. I'm just one person, but then again, so is Shand. Perhaps you're more like me in this regard, or perhaps you're more like Shand. If you're more like me, you're probably already more worried about the tangible dangers of underthinking than about the putative dangers of overthinking.

But if you're more like Shand, perhaps I can say something to alleviate the worry. In fact, let me try two approaches. First, any kind of "love" that would not survive a long, close look may not be such a wonderful thing to have in your life after all. Things that disappear when you look too closely often were never there in the first place: that's how illusions and tricks of the eye work. Perhaps you're thinking you'd rather be blissfully unaware, but ignorance is no guarantee of bliss. Illusions are unstable things that can crumble for all sorts of reasons and without warning, even if you studiously avoid looking at them.

Here's a second reason not to be afraid of philosophizing about love. Philosophy is about forming one's own opinions through careful thought, not absorbing someone else's. I don't expect you to agree with me about love by the end of this book. But that aside, I won't be trying to convince you that love is unreal, or contradictory, or illusory. My philosophical thinking suggests romantic love is very real, and I don't think we were ever in any danger of analyzing it out of existence. Love is complicated and confusing, sure, and we need to sort out a number of philosophical problems about it. But the theory I'm offering is a theory of a real thing. In the end I am not cynical about love, though I would say I am careful. But it's important to be careful. Love is an extreme sport, and we don't skydive without parachutes.

In my work, I am influenced by a tradition in philosophy known as analytic metaphysics. Metaphysics is philosophical inquiry into what reality is like, and analytic metaphysics aims to proceed in such inquiry by deploying careful, rigorous argumentation and critical reasoning. Analytic philosophy has roots in the work of thinkers like Bertrand Russell, G. E. Moore, and Ludwig Wittgenstein, who were prominent professors of philosophy at Trinity College, Cambridge, during the early twentieth century. As I studied philosophy at Trinity College during the 1990s and early 2000s, this tradition heavily influenced my intellectual development.

Analytic metaphysicians spend their working lives attempting to better understand the nature of reality. We try to be careful in our thinking and clear in our writing and to question assumptions however "natural" they feel. These days, not very many analytic metaphysicians are working on love. But I think this is just a kind of historical accident: analytic metaphysics has trends and fashions, and the metaphysics of love hasn't been fashionable lately. But love occupies the entire careers of other scholars, artists, writers, and thinkers. I've been influenced by much more of that intellectual heritage than I could ever discuss in a short book; choosing material to include was more like curating an interesting exhibition than composing a definitive index.

Whatever the current trends, Bertrand Russell—a founder of analytic philosophy—had plenty to say about love, sex, and marriage. Engaging his analytic skills, he stood ready to challenge the prevailing assumptions on these subjects and tried to follow evidence and reasons where they led. His conclusions were so radical that he eventually lost a university position in the United States after being pronounced "morally unfit" for the job. Radical thinking is not always the safest or most comfortable life choice.

My training gave me a set of techniques: a toolkit for careful, rigorous, honest thinking—not the only such toolkit, but a powerful one. Used to its fullest potential, it can be radical, and it can be costly. But I wouldn't—couldn't—trade it in for an unquestioning mind. That carries its own costs, and in my estimation they are much higher.

This book, then, is an invitation for you to join me at the front lines of the philosophy of love. It comes with a starter kit: philosophical ideas, strategies, arguments, and theories. You might find you agree or disagree with what I say, but it is in that very process of agreeing and disagreeing that philosophers develop and refine ideas, pushing the questions a little further and deeper with each step in the conversation. Philosophy is a massive, ongoing, collaborative human enterprise, and I hope you join it.

For my part in this collaboration, in this book I offer my own theory of love. The main idea is that romantic love has a dual nature. Right now, we are witnessing the simultaneous development of convincing social and biological theories of what love is. Theories that make love a social or cultural construct of some kind have been around for a while, albeit with significant variation and development. Biological theories feel like a newer phenomenon, and, indeed, in their current incarnations they are new, though they have older precedents. But recent work in neuroscience makes it possible to construct a biological theory of love with genuine plausibility. And the arrival on the scene of viable biological theories of love forces a question: Is romantic love really a social construct or a biological phenomenon? At this point, our two theories of love become an embarrassment of riches. We start with the question, What is love? We're told that love is biology. We're also told that love is society. That sounds like one answer too many.

Of course, we could just pick one. There's a problem with that, though, serious enough to turn this choice into a dilemma: making a straight choice amounts to losing half of our accumulated knowledge and wisdom. That would be foolhardy for sure. Yet if we don't make a choice, we seem to be left with an incoherent mess in our metaphysics. With all this going on, no wonder we're confused.

I believe the conceptual tools needed to resolve this situation are available to us. Inspired by philosophical work in other areas, I have come to believe in a theory of love that can weave our embarrassment of riches into a coherent picture. The key is to show how social and biological accounts of love are not really in competition but are complementary descriptions of a complex reality: love has a dual nature.

I suspect the failure to identify love's dual nature is responsible for much of our intellectual puzzlement about love. Even more worryingly, I suspect that it serves as a significant barrier to progress. Torn between the biological and social conceptions, we can easily fall back into the comforting arms of the romantic mystique, accepting love without understanding or challenging it. We may be held back from social critique by a niggling sense that love is a "natural," biological phenomenon and, as such, not a suitable subject for such critique. Yet, at the very same time, we may be held back in attempts to gain and disseminate a strong scientific understanding of love by a niggling sense that love is a cultural (or perhaps totally magical or incomprehensible) phenomenon and, as such, not a suitable subject for scientific inquiry.

In reality, neither concern should impede either project. Armed with the correct understanding of love's dual nature, biological and social theories of love can progress in tandem. They can inform and strengthen one another. We can have conversations about love that cross disciplinary boundaries in a way that unites rather than divides our various intellectual enterprises. In fact, we urgently need to do all this in order to make conscious and informed decisions about love. What do we want romantic love to look like ten years from now, or twenty, or fifty? We must ask ourselves this question and act on the answer. We have to understand that the future of love is in our hands and that we have a responsibility to get this right. We can only undertake positive change as a collective enterprise, and empowering ourselves with the tools to think clearly about love is the essential first step.

In the later chapters of this book, after outlining my theory, I will sketch some of the ways the social aspect of love's nature is changing over time. I'll explore how we might want love to change—socially and perhaps even biologically—from what it is now. I'll talk about what it would take to move toward some of the practical, intellectual, and social benefits that I believe are within reach once we understand the dual nature of love.

As for what kind of book this is, perhaps it helps to start by saying what it's not. It's not relationship advice, self-help, or a collection of anecdotes. It's not an attempt to popularize science; nor is it an academic tome. And it's certainly not a survey or summary of all extant thinking about love. None of those would be a way of achieving what I'm trying to achieve (and the last one is impossible).

I could call this book an exercise in critical thinking out loud, but it's important to explain why I'm doing it *out loud*. Why does it matter if you read it? Because we need a conversation, not a monologue. This conversation we need to have, about the nature of romantic love, is one of the most significant and urgent cultural projects of our shared moment in time. So much so that I am sometimes tempted to think of this book as "self-help" for a culture (rather than for individuals). When we, as a society, can come to a better understanding of what love is, we will be better able to take control of how love treats us in the future.

So I am inviting you to be an active reader: not to passively absorb my ideas but to question, challenge, and ultimately push these investigations far beyond anything I can imagine right now. I can't "do" the philosophy of love by myself; no one can.

Ready to get started?

1

Love Is Biology

What is your substance, whereof are you made,
That millions of strange shadows on you tend?

—William Shakespeare, Sonnet 53

Dismantling the Romantic Mystique

There is a lot to be said for thinking of ourselves as human animals: a naturally occurring biological phenomenon, amenable to scientific investigation like any other. Much of modern medicine owes its success to thinking of ourselves that way, and the dramatic increases in life expectancy and quality of life that have accompanied medical advancement make a pretty compelling case for this conception of what we are.

That said, it's not surprising that romantic love—with all its poetic and magical associations—should be a holdout against the rising tide of naturalistic self-interpretation. The poet John

Keats, writing in the early nineteenth century, held science responsible for the loss of the world's magic. (In keeping with his time, he calls science "philosophy": science and philosophy were not separated into distinct enterprises until later.) His sentiments strike a chord with many even today, when he says, "Philosophy will clip an Angel's wings" and "unweave a rainbow."[1] For some people, romantic love has pride of place among a dwindling stock of intact rainbows.

But there are risks inherent in treating love as an inexplicable mystery. The analogy with medicine shows why. If we want a good standard of medical care, we need medical science based on a solid grasp of human biology. That's not all we need for good medical care, but it is necessary. We can't achieve this knowledge if we treat our bodies as inexplicable and mysterious. If we don't even try to understand how our bodies work, we won't know how to fix them when they are broken. Romantic love is the same.

Recent developments in the biology of love are providing valuable insights into how love works. Writers E. B. and K. S. White once quipped, "Humor can be dissected, as a frog can, but the thing dies in the process and the innards are discouraging to any but the pure scientific mind."[2] Some might say the same is true of love, but they would be mistaken. There is actually huge public demand for scientific information about love; its "innards" appear to be the opposite of discouraging. Moreover, this fascination has not left everyone's relationships dead on the dissecting table.

In any case, there is no mileage to gain in standing at the the rising tide of science, yelling at it to turn back and not dampen the gorgeous robes of poetry and magic we have dressed love up in. Scientists will continue to advance our understanding of love, whether we cheer them on or mourn the magic lost in the process. For what it's worth, I'll be among those doing the cheering. I think a better scientific understanding of love can help make us safer, healthier, and more aware of who and what we are.

Love's Biology

That doesn't mean we should just accept everything any scientist tells us about love. While I am fundamentally convinced of the need for a biological theory, many of the particular claims presented under the aegis of "biology" are suspect. As philosophers, we must approach the biology of love with both interest and caution.

Helen Fisher is one of the most influential contemporary theorists of romantic love, which she treats as a thoroughly biological phenomenon. Fisher is a researcher, author, public speaker, and advisor to online dating service Match.com. Her work is a perfect spark for discussing the biology of love, and as such I'll address it in some detail. But many other influential contemporary thinkers are also approaching love from the perspective of biology. For example, *Sex at Dawn* by Christopher Ryan and Cacilda Jethá has recently made a big impact on discussions of sex, romance, and relationships by framing these topics in terms of what is "natural" for our species given our biological makeup and evolutionary past.[3] And this is not happening in a cultural or intellectual vacuum: the hope that biology can answer fundamental questions about us has been quite prevalent for some time, although it is perennially controversial.

The basic idea that romantic love is a biological phenomenon is not new. Precedents stretch back to the ancient world (of which more later). More recently, Renaissance medicine attributed "amorous" dispositions and "love-melancholy" to an imbalance in bodily fluids (the four humors). More recently still, philosopher Arthur Schopenhauer claimed that "romantic love" was just a grandiose label for sexual desire, itself a mere prompt to biological reproduction. The contemporary work of theorists like Fisher differs in that we may now be able to start getting the biology right. It's easy to see in retrospect that medicine based on the four humors was quackery and that Schopenhauer was an angry pessimist motivated by an alarming ideological agenda (one that included misogyny and homophobia). But Fisher is a serious researcher who's actually doing the science; work like hers we cannot dismiss so easily. It's one thing to say love is biology of some kind or other. It's a whole different ball game to step up and say love consists of these specific biological mechanisms and here is the science to prove it.

Fisher's work is a great starting point for discussion because it provides a clear, explicit, and—most importantly—credible contemporary development of the idea that love is biology. Fisher thinks romantic love is literally identical to a biological drive, one identifiable by means of its evolutionary history and its role within the human body (and specifically the brain). So let's explore in a bit more detail what she says romantic love is and why.

What Drives Us

In her influential book *Why We Love: The Nature and Chemistry of Romantic Love,* Fisher discusses experiments that she and various collaborators conducted on individuals who said they had recently fallen intensely in love.[4] Using functional magnetic resonance imaging (fMRI) scans, they found that these individuals showed elevated activity in the caudate nucleus and ventral tegmental area, regions associated with the brain's reward system. Fisher reports finding that the reward-related neurotransmitter dopamine appeared to be implicated in producing some of the activities characteristic of intense romantic love, such as obsessive focus and energy directed at the beloved. There is also some evidence (though Fisher does not emphasize this) for the involvement of cortisol in the early stages of romantic love. Cortisol is associated with arousal and stress generally.[5]

The role of dopamine, however, is highly significant for Fisher: it supports her view that romantic love is "a fundamental human drive," like our need for food and water (so, she adds, is the "maternal instinct"). Fisher thinks love is a basic biological urge that motivates us to do things that we as a species need to do in order to survive and thrive. She reasons that "all of the basic drives are associated with elevated levels of dopamine," and so she counts the involvement of dopamine in romantic love as evidence that romantic love is likewise a basic drive. According to Fisher, it is in fact "one of three primordial brain networks that evolved to direct mating and reproduction": lust, romantic love, and attachment. She reports that each of these "travels along different pathways in the brain" and is "associated with different neurochemicals." Lust, she says, is associated primarily with testosterone, romantic love with dopamine, and attachment with oxytocin and vasopressin.

Now, even if we want to accept a theory in this vicinity, there are some lurking philosophical questions concerning whether love should be identified with a *drive*, as Fisher suggests, or with (say) the brain states or neurochemical cocktails that result from that drive's activation. But I'm not going to worry about details like that for the purposes of this book.[6] I find much more relevant Fisher's separation of attachment from romantic love. My dispute with this might be verbal, but even so, it is one that matters. (Words, in general, matter.) Fisher's taxonomy is misleading: her vocabulary is a mismatch for the way we usually talk about romantic love. An adequate, comprehensive theory of romantic love will need to cover many cases of what Fisher classifies as "attachment." Stable, calm, attached love should not fail to count as romantic just because it is stable and calm, rather than intense and passionate like the early-stage, dopamine-driven phenomenon that Fisher identifies as "romantic" love. Indeed, the love at the end of some of the most "romantic" stories I know is the stable, calm kind.

Renowned philosopher Robert Nozick, writing in the 1980s, thought of romantic love as going through two phases: an initial intense phase and a subsequent stable phase.[7] While best known for his political philosophy, Nozick was also philosophically interested in romantic love, which he thought of as a desire for a certain kind of union with another person. He theorized that in its first stage, this desire would manifest as intense and passionate, while in its second stage, after the formation of the desired union, it would become settled and stable. Nozick's two-stage theory resonates with many,[8] but it represents a disagreement with Fisher, who appears to classify only the first phase as "romantic" love. She would label the second phase something else: "attachment" love.

I disagree with Fisher: attachment love can be romantic love. But that's not to say I agree with Nozick's two-stage view, at least not as a universal theory. It seems possible for romantic love to be calm and stable from the outset; why not? Not all relationships have to begin with passion and fireworks: sometimes old friends gradually and peacefully realize that they are more than just friends. This shouldn't disqualify theirs from counting as romantic love. It also seems possible for romantic love to be intense for its entire duration and to never settle down. And who's to say romantic love can't end up alternating back and forth between periods of calm and periods of intensity? Romantic love is not one-size-fits-all, and an adequate theory simply has to deal with this. Both Fisher and Nozick are trying to make a very diverse phenomenon fit the confines of too narrow a mold.

Anyhow, given that romantic love can sometimes take the form of what Fisher would call "attachment," we need to include the science of attachment if we want to understand the science of romantic love in general. In this connection, Fisher and others have emphasized the role of the hormones oxytocin and vasopressin and of the brain region known as the hypothalamus, which—along with the ovaries and testes—generates the relevant hormones in the human body.

Where Does <u>Love</u> Come From?

To match her biological theory of what love is, Fisher offers a biological account of where it came from. (Spoiler: evolution.) She writes, "Each brain system evolved to direct a different aspect of reproduction. Lust evolved to motivate individuals to seek sexual union with almost *any* semi-appropriate partner. Romantic love emerged to drive men and women to focus their mating attention on a preferred individual. . . . And the brain circuitry for male-female attachment developed to enable our ancestors to live with this mate at least long enough to rear a single child through infancy together."

She later expands on this idea, saying that the arrival of bipedalism in our evolutionary history "caused a problem for females: they became obliged to carry their babies in their arms instead of on their backs." And so they "began to need mates to help feed and protect them—at least while they carried and nursed a child." Fisher proposes this as the evolutionary explanation for pair-bonding—and hence romantic love—in our species. She reasons that because a female would need a male to provide for her, pair-bonding became "essential" for females. And she figures a male couldn't protect or provide for a "harem" of females, so pair-bonding also became "practical" for males. We know the end of the story: "monogamy—the human habit of forming a pair-bond with one individual at a time—evolved."

There is a lot of philosophical work to be done here. For one thing, we need to appreciate the impact of the heteronormative culture within which Fisher is working, and I'll come back to this later. For now, I want to make an initial separation between two things that come wrapped up together in Fisher's work: the fascinating *scientific results* she is discussing (and has herself been at the forefront of achieving) and her *metaphysical theorizing* as to the nature of romantic love. The latter is a branch of philosophy, and in general scientific expertise does not guarantee that one's philosophical theories will be correct.

The scientific results Fisher reports include things like the observations obtained by means of fMRI scans revealing that certain areas of the brain are more active in individuals who report being newly and intensely in love. The philosophical theorizing takes over when Fisher goes on to say that romantic love is, of its essence, a basic biological drive that evolved because our helpless female ancestors needed monogamous males to provide for them while they reared their babies.

Of course, Fisher's results and her theorizing are connected: she takes her results to be evidence for her philosophical theory. "Our results changed my thinking about the very essence of romantic love," as she puts it. For example, as we saw, she points to the involvement of dopamine in both romantic love and all (other) basic human drives as a reason to believe that love is itself a basic human drive. But as philosophers we must bear in mind that, along with data, personal and cultural experiences in the arena of love are—inevitably—also part of what goes into the act of theorizing about love. Fisher, like anybody, is much more likely to believe in a theory of love that is consonant with her own experiences.

This is not a criticism: it is reasonable and rational to be more favorably inclined toward a theory that makes sense of one's own experiences. And there is simply no way for us to be inquirers—whether that amounts to being a philosopher, a biologist, an anthropologist, or simply a curious person—without also being humans. We bring our humanity and our experience to all our intellectual pursuits, and these impact how we proceed in those pursuits. The real risk is not that this will happen but that if we ignore it—if we downplay the involvement of the personal and the cultural in the intellectual—we are ignoring some of the most powerful factors that shape the work of scientists, philosophers, and everyone else.

I find Fisher's philosophical theory unconvincing in part because it is so dissonant with experiences of love drawn from my life and the lives of people I know. I'll say more about this later. For now, it's enough to note that we don't have to agree with all the details of Fisher's metaphysical theorizing about love to appreciate why her scientific work is important. It is very hard to deny that the results she has identified tell us something significant about the biological nature of love. So let's focus for a moment on what that is.

What Is Real

The big idea motivating Fisher—a biological theory of romantic love based on isolating the neurochemistry and neurophysiology involved—is on the right track. If we want to understand what love is, we will need to listen to the people studying our bodies and brains in controlled and data-driven ways that can be tested, peer-reviewed, reproduced, and verified and that deliver measurable results. We will need to learn the science of love. We should respect science's successful track record in bringing us to a better understanding of ourselves. Reading the experimental work conducted by Fisher and others, I find it hard to resist the pull toward concluding that romantic love is something natural, biological, and scientifically investigable: something "hardwired" into our biology and brain chemistry, ready to be triggered under certain circumstances, with the full force of an evolutionary history behind it.

If this is right, there are limits to how fully we will ever understand love just by studying culture, literature, or art. If love is a biological phenomenon, the scientific method has the right credentials for investigating such a thing. Mapping cultural trends in love, however fascinating in other ways, will not give us the necessary grasp of love's biological profile. Biology got there first: our dopamine and cortisol responses were developing long before anything like the complex structure of contemporary society existed. And biology persists through cultural change: attitudes and opinions about love come and go, but our brain circuitry stays relatively constant across the centuries. All of this means that we need to understand the biology of love not just for formulating a proper theory of what love is now but also for thinking about what love has been in the past and what it could be in the future.

Moreover, while brain circuitry is relatively stable over time, we are acquiring new ways of interfering with it as our knowledge advances. Ethicists and scientists are already debating the possible impacts of medical interventions that may be able to alter how, when, or even whether love occurs. Certain drugs may be able to enhance or encourage the biological responses

characteristic of love, while others—sometimes called "chemical breakup" drugs—may be able to lessen or prevent these
responses. This isn't wild science fiction; it is already a realistic
possibility. For example, testosterone, oxytocin, and vasopressin
are being discussed as drugs that might increase the likelihood of
love occurring or continuing,[9] while antagonists for oxytocin, vasopressin, or dopamine are being considered as ways of reducing
that likelihood.[10]

In the future it may be possible to intervene in the biology of
love in yet more dramatic ways. There is evidence that *epigenetic*
effects (environmental influences on gene expression, which are
sometimes heritable) can be used to regulate pair-bonding in
mammals. In prairie voles, for example, certain epigenetic mechanisms have been found to enhance pair-bonding (in the absence
of a more usual mechanism, sex).[11] Perhaps one day we'll be able
to manipulate human pair-bonding in similar ways. Perhaps we'll
be able to alter the composition of our own brains so as to render
ourselves incapable of love. Perhaps we'll bring falling in and out
of love under total control, rendering it as simple as opening and
closing an app on our smartphones.

Should medical interventions to encourage or suppress love
be permitted? Should they be regulated? Would it devalue love to
know that it had been artificially enhanced?[12] Would we stand to
lose something valuable—opportunities for learning or personal
growth, maybe—by exercising chemical control at love's most
difficult moments? Would it be worth paying that price to avoid
the misery of intense long-term feelings for inappropriate or
abusive partners? What about using drugs to get over someone
who is just not that into you?

We need to be having conversations about these issues, and I'll circle back to some of them near the end of this book. But the salient point here is that we need to understand the biology of love even to get as far as figuring out what questions to ask about all of this. That's one reason why appreciating the biological nature of love is important: it empowers us to think clearly about the future of love, balancing what we want to do against what we actually can do.

Cocktail Recipes

We first need to appreciate that, at the biological level, love exhibits significant variation. Even Fisher, one of the most prominent advocates of a biological theory of love, is not saying that the biology of love looks exactly the same in everyone. The data tell us that there are statistically significant correlations between reported experiences of romantic love and things like heightened activity in certain areas of the brain or elevated levels of certain brain chemicals. But exactly how much activity in which areas and exactly how much of which chemicals—all this is subject to interpersonal variation.

You might hear love described metaphorically as "a cocktail of chemicals." But if love is a cocktail, it has no single, strict recipe. It's better conceived of as a family of cocktails. Consider daiquiris. You'd expect to find a few basic ingredients in a daiquiri: some kind of rum, some sort of citrus juice (usually lime), and some sort of sweetener (usually sugar). But individual daiquiris vary the ratios, and some include other ingredients like strawberries or bananas. Other daiquiris get creative and replace the rum with another spirit.

The brain chemistry for love is similarly variable. What's more, there's nothing at all surprising about this. All humans belong to a single species, but we differ in the details of our biological makeup. We exhibit variation in all kinds of traits, from obvious things like eye color and arm length to less obvious things like fingerprints and DNA. There is no one way to have a human biology. Romantic love is no exception to the rule.

Just as in the biology of love, in the psychology of love we see significant diversity between individuals. To pick just one type of example, researchers recently found that in two samples of long-term married couples, 29 and 40 percent of participants reported still being "very intensely in love" after more than ten years of marriage.[13] The study identified correlations with various other psychological and behavioral factors. Another study found that reports of long-term intense romantic love correlated with certain patterns of brain activity.[14]

These findings are intriguingly in tension with the philosophical theory of love offered by Robert Nozick. Remember that he said romantic love is a two-stage business: it passes through a brief, passionate first stage to reach a long-term, calm second stage. The first stage (which Nozick calls "infatuation") is supposed to transform into continuing love or else disappear. But someone who feels "very intensely" in love after ten years of marriage doesn't fit comfortably into either of Nozick's two boxes.

Interpersonal variation is no barrier to proper scientific understanding, however. In fact, when carefully handled, the science of love serves to protect us against making unscientific overgeneralizations that float free of empirical data. The scientific method, properly applied, cautions us not to overinterpret the limited data we have.

Science Will Save Us

Isn't there something intellectually comforting about the idea that science can finally tell us what love really is? Isn't it reassuring to think we might finally get some answers, through the application of tried and trusted experimental methods, to our deepest and most perplexing questions about love? It is to me. Love can make people behave in such strange ways and exerts such a formative influence in so many people's lives. Yet it's been treated as irredeemably mysterious for so long that we've come to regard bafflement as a normal state of affairs. It is awfully tempting—and not unrealistic—to hope that science will finally dispel the romantic mystique.

The kinds of answers we get from the science of love really do seem to explain a lot when it comes to things like the strange behaviors that love can induce. Studies are revealing important biochemical similarities between the brains of people who are intensely in love and those of people experiencing chemical addiction. Fisher describes some of these results in a TED talk titled "The Brain in Love," in which she explains how she and her colleagues found that romantic love is linked with activity in the ventral tegmental area, particularly the A10 cells, which make dopamine. She refers to this as part of the "reptilian core of the brain, associated with wanting, with motivation, with focus, and with craving." As she points out, the very same brain region also gets activated during a cocaine rush.[15]

A biological approach to the nature of love has a lot going for it. It promises relatively clear and straightforward answers to the old question, What is love? We could say love is a kind of neurochemical cocktail (or, better, family of cocktails). Or we could say—with Fisher—that love is a basic drive, like hunger or thirst, that evolved in our evolutionary past to use these chemical cocktails to get us to behave in ways that promoted the survival of our species. These biological theories offer real explanatory value and help make sense of what people in love go through: love can feel like addiction because it can biochemically resemble addiction. Love is powerfully motivating because it evolved for an important purpose. We can rigorously test and refine the information on which this kind of theory rests, using methodologies that have proven their value in many areas of science. On top of all that, the biological approach to love has important practical implications: when discussing how we might want love to change, particularly when it comes to using biochemical interventions to encourage or suppress love, we have to start out with a good grasp of love's biological nature or we'll be wasting our breath.

Will Science Save Us?

And yet . . . there's an "and yet." Taking a purely biological approach to love raises some tricky issues. For starters, we need to ask a few questions about methodology. Current scientific research on romantic love relies heavily on self-reporting: when selecting study participants who are "in love," researchers take their cue from what people tell them. This can be a problem, as people might not be fully accurate, honest, or consistent in this kind of self-reporting for all kinds of reasons—some idiosyncratic, some systematic; some deliberate, some unintentional.[16]

There are also philosophical concerns that run deeper than method. If we say that love is biology—literally a feature of our biological makeup—then we appear to be committed to saying that any creature with a radically different makeup from ours cannot be in love. Maybe other animals with enough similarities in their evolutionary pasts could be candidates, but we would be ruling out the possibility of an artificially intelligent computer or robot falling in love: regardless of how sophisticated the technology becomes, computers and robots would not share enough of our biology or evolutionary history. By the lights of a biological theory of love, the plot of the movie *Her*—in which a man seems to fall in love with his computer operating system (OS) and vice versa—would be no more than a story about a deeply confused individual. His OS cannot love him: an OS is incapable of love because it is not a biological organism, and love is a biological phenomenon.

Maybe that sounds just right to you: perhaps you agree that a computer OS could not be in love. But what about other possible creatures with very different biologies and evolutionary histories? What about aliens? Or what about designer life forms that didn't evolve at all but were brought into existence through direct human agency? If love is indeed a feature of human biology, then all these other creatures can never be in love. Now perhaps you're not too worried about aliens and designer life forms either: after all, we don't exactly bump into them on a daily basis. But do we really want a theory of love to tie our hands on these questions about what's possible? Do we want to buy into a theory that limiting before all the facts are in about what we might encounter in the future?

Maybe a biological theorist of love can do some fancy philosophical footwork and find a way to avoid these theoretical constraints. These issues arise in other areas of philosophy too—for example, in the investigation of what pain is—and metaphysicians of the mind are already at work developing ingenious solutions. But another serious issue lurks: a purely biological theory of romantic love doesn't properly accommodate the role of culture and society. A purely biological theory predicts that cultural influences play a negligible to nonexistent role in determining the nature of romantic love. Our biology is not in any substantial way a product of society or culture. So if love is part of our biology, love is not in any substantial way a product of society or culture.

This would mean we must reject claims like "Romantic love has changed a lot over the last few hundred years and is still changing" or "Romantic love differs radically between cultures." Ancient, evolved brain chemistry and fundamental human drives don't differ radically among cultures and don't change much in the space of a few hundred years. So why does romantic love seem to vary so much across time and across cultures if it is a biological phenomenon? This is the one big question to which a simple biological theory of love cannot give any answer that I would find satisfying. The theory predicts some individual variation in different people's cocktail recipes for love, but biology alone cannot adequately explain these large-scale variations that look like they are tracking cultural differences.

A biological theory of love can be intellectually satisfying in a number of ways and practically important for making informed ethical choices. But if you're anything like me, it just doesn't feel like the whole story. In the next chapter I expand on the themes of change and intercultural variation as I examine the case for saying that romantic love is not a biological phenomenon after all but rather a socially constructed one.

Love Is Society

LOVE, n. *A temporary insanity curable by marriage or by removal of the patient from the influences under which he incurred the disorder. This disease, like caries and many other ailments, is prevalent only among civilized races living under artificial conditions; barbarous nations breathing pure air and eating simple food enjoy immunity from its ravages. It is sometimes fatal, but more frequently to the physician than to the patient.*

—Ambrose Bierce, *The Devil's Dictionary*

Let's Just Talk

Not even an introvert like me exists in a social vacuum. The society around us constantly shapes and influences everything we think, say, and do. This influence often goes unnoticed; it tends to make its presence felt only when we start resisting it in some way. But noticed or not, it is real, and its effects are powerful. In many ways we are artifacts of culture.

When I talk publicly about having two partners, people often react by trying to reinforce the cultural norm of monogamy that I've broken. Some call me horrible names in anonymous comments or messages, attempting to shore up that norm. Others remind me that I'm not "normal" in subtler ways: unprompted declarations that they "could never do that," for example, or reminders that my life is "an experiment" (as if anyone's isn't). But I want to talk about the power of the unsubtle for a moment. Let's think about the word "slut."

The meaning of the word "slut" encodes a socially significant idea: that promiscuous women are bad. The word packs together a description (promiscuous woman) and an evaluation (bad). This means that when you use this word uncritically, you commit yourself to that value judgment: that is, you signal to the world that you think promiscuous women are bad. Of course, the meanings of words can change, and some pejoratives and slurs get reclaimed over time, losing their negative connotations. But "slut" retains much of its negative charge, despite some efforts at reclamation.

I mention this because language is a great case study in how our mechanisms for transmitting socially significant information are simultaneously effective and invisible. When we learn a language as children, we do not critically assess each new word, think through all the consequences of using it, and decide whether or not we approve of those consequences. We just imitate the people around us. We just talk. But learning the word "slut" at an early age will influence our perception of women for the rest of our lives. As any advertiser will tell you, a name can change everything. A rose by the name "poo-petals" would not smell as sweet.[1] But most people never notice how the language they speak prescribes their worldview.

Slurs are among the more obvious examples of how language shapes our understanding, but all sorts of language can be used to encode social information, transmitting and reinforcing cultural values. Indeed, the very fact that we even have a word for something provides an implicit signal that it is worth talking about. The effects of lacking words to describe one's own experiences can be serious. For example, lacking a word like "polyamorous," a polyamorous person can be left reaching for words that encode a negative judgment (such as "unfaithful") or suggest a crime or sin (such as "adulterous"). Only being able to describe your intimate feelings by passing negative judgment on yourself has psychological consequences.

The worldviews encoded in our language are handed to us through the social mechanism of language learning, so what we get depends on the particular social context we happen to find ourselves in when we are acquiring language. It's a bit of a lottery.

What Have We Created?

Language is just one of a suite of powerful tools that societies use to transmit information and reinforce values. We are also permanently imbibing the art, politics, institutions, laws, practices, and traditions of the culture within which we are embedded. We have been taking all this in by osmosis since our earliest childhood, and it's now practically impossible to think outside all of these boxes, even if we try. They are such a normal and continuous part of life that they seem completely "natural" to us. It's no coincidence that we use this word—"natural"—to describe the utterly familiar: familiarity makes it so easy to mistake culture for nature.

Romantic love is a perfect example of how society shapes our sense of what is "natural." In this chapter I discuss the theory that romantic love is a *social construct*—something society has created—rather than a feature of biology. I look at reasons for denying that romantic love is a human universal (at least in any straightforward way): despite what the biological theory of love would have us believe, there are good reasons for treating romantic love as a relatively recent, localized phenomenon, one that varies significantly among cultures because they construct it differently.

To think our way into these ideas, let's consider ancient Greece for a moment. In ancient Greece, marriage was largely about procreation and the controlled inheritance of property. It was treated as a kind of transaction in which fathers could present their daughters to prospective grooms as gifts, prizes, or rewards. (Today the practice of fathers' symbolically or ceremonially "giving away" brides to their husbands echoes this conception of marriage.) As Western European society changed, romantic love took over the institution of marriage. Contemporary weddings in Western Europe and North America usually come with a presumption that love brought the couple together, not a financial arrangement between men.

Now here's a way of interpreting this change. As a new social arrangement emerged in Western European culture, a new role gradually opened up: a place in social life for a kind of love distinctively related to marriage. A need had arisen for a kind of love that would bring couples together in a monogamous, lifelong, nuclear family–like bond, replacing the work previously done by patriarchal financial arrangements.

Seen that way, a view of romantic love as defined by its role in this new social setup starts to make sense: it appeared because we had created certain specific work for it to do. Of course, various other kinds of love were around already; we're talking about how *romantic* love (as we know it) came to exist. The ancient Greeks had several words for different kinds of love, including *eros*, *agape*, and *philia*. *Eros* is often translated as "passionate love" or "desire"; *agape* is usually taken to refer to a kind of brotherly love (interpreted in some Christian traditions as the love of God for us and vice versa); and *philia* is a kind of friendly affection. But romantic love isn't exactly any of these, although it can include components of each. *Eros* is perhaps the best contender, but romantic love need not always be passionate (or "erotic" in the modern sense). And a pure sexual lust could count as a form of *eros* but would not count as romantic love.

The idea that romantic love is a social construct is part of a broader intellectual movement that pushes back against our temptation to attribute to biology things that are really the products of social institutions, practices, and traditions. This movement stretches across contemporary debates about the nature of gender, race, disability, orientation, and other things. A social constructionist about gender, for example, might say that gender is not a feature of a person's "natural" biological makeup; it is rather a matter of conforming (or being expected to conform) to certain norms around behavior, dress, self-presentation, social roles, and so on. Gender, in this constructionist picture, is created when we as a society decide to bundle together these norms and attach them to biological markers (such as genitalia or chromosomes). While a gender may be assigned to a child at birth on a presumed biological basis—say, based on the child's having "male" or "female" genitalia—the social constructionist maintains that gender itself is no part of the child's biology. This offers one possible explanation for how some trans* people can be assigned a gender that does not match their gender identity.

A social constructionist about romantic love may hold, correspondingly, that romantic love is a product of social expectations, traditions, and norms rather than a biological phenomenon. Love might be associated with biological markers—once identifiable as fuzzy feelings of excitement or warmth, now traceable to the involvement of dopamine or oxytocin—but the constructionist says these biological markers are not what romantic love truly is.

So what exactly is romantic love for a social constructionist? Well, it depends on which constructionist you ask. But just as Helen Fisher gave us a clear example of a biological theory, two psychologists—Anne Beall and Robert Sternberg—offer a clear example of a social constructionist theory. So let's take a look at what they think love is and why.

It Takes a Village to Fall in Love

In 1995 Beall and Sternberg published a paper titled "The Social Construction of Love."[2] In this work they say they find it "difficult, if not impossible," to address the question of what romantic love is because "any answer must reflect its time period and place, and in particular, the functions that romantic love serves there." In other words, whatever the biological theorists might say, there is no hope of a once-and-for-all answer. Love varies among cultures. And Beall and Sternberg don't just mean that it gets described or expressed differently: they mean the actual phenomenon—the experience of love itself—varies. (Culture certainly affects how we express love, but that by itself would be no challenge to the idea that love's nature is biological. After all, culture also affects how we express hunger and pain.)

To give one example inspired by their discussion, consider a woman falling in love in Victorian England. The idea is that she will literally *go through a different process* compared to a woman falling in love in contemporary Canada. For the Victorian lady, falling in love is a matter of developing a deep and respectful (but probably rather distant) admiration for a man. Sexual desire is at best irrelevant to this process, at worst a shameful distraction. For the contemporary Canadian, however, falling in love is a matter of developing an intimate attachment that normatively includes sexual desire. If sexual desire is absent, that is at best noticeably unusual; at worst it is interpreted as showing that the feelings involved are not romantic but platonic.

According to the constructionist theory, this is a difference in the actual phenomenon of romantic love, not just how love gets expressed. But notice that even variation in the phenomenon itself doesn't yet prove that love is a social construct. After all, two different cultural groups might vary with regard to how fast their fingernails grew for genetic or environmental reasons; rate of nail growth would still be a biological feature and not a socially constructed one. The key point is that genetics and environment don't offer any obvious explanation for the differences between Victorian love and contemporary love. While variation across cultures does not entail social constructionism, it provides evidence for it when the best or only explanation of that variation is that different societies are constructing different things.

As Beall and Sternberg put it, "There is not one particular 'reality' that is simultaneously experienced by all people." When it comes to love, people "are not passive recipients of a set of events" but "are actively constructing social information." This is their constructionist conclusion. There is also the alternative of attributing mass error: we could say that one culture has romantic love truly figured out, and everyone else is getting it wrong. But I don't see any legitimate reason for privileging one culture's ideas about love in this way, taking them alone to track reality. (In particular, I don't think biology gives us any reason to privilege one culture's ideas about love; I'll say more about this later.)

It is also significant that the kinds of variation love exhibits are major and quite central to the whole idea of what love is—indeed, who we are. They do not reflect mere tinkering around the edges of a kind we could easily attribute to misunderstandings or differences of expression. Beall and Sternberg present a wealth of examples of large-scale cultural variation as evidence to support their constructionist view. We've already seen how romantic love was not always sexualized: Victorian culture commonly conceived of love as lofty, admirable, and asexual, while it viewed sex quite negatively. During the Enlightenment, romantic love was seen as rational (or at least potentially under rational control), while the Romantics saw it as uncontrollable and tumultuous. The treatment of love as the basis for marriage and family formation is a recent development in cultures of European origin. And some older work cited by Beall and Sternberg suggests that the kind of romantic love construed as "normal" in contemporary US culture would more likely seem "aberrant" from the perspective of Chinese culture. Beall and Sternberg diagnose this last difference by contrasting what they perceive as American individualism— with its emphasis on emotional self-expression—with what they characterize as a Chinese cultural emphasis on family and social relations. (It is worth bearing in mind, however, that they were writing in 1995 and citing research from the 1980s. Attitudes toward this kind of difference have become more sophisticated over time, as researchers veer away from dealing in monolithic cultural stereotypes.)

Beall and Sternberg also explain how these differing social standards shape individual experiences: people regulate their own experiences of love, and those of others around them, by encouraging favored manifestations and discouraging others in accordance with the norms of their social setting. The resultant phenomenon is, in many ways, a far cry from anything "hardwired" in us by nature or biology.

Society Versus Biology

Supposing love is indeed a social construct, what should we say about biology? Beall and Sternberg do not entirely deny its relevance, but they mention it only in passing: "We can presume love includes [a biological] component," they say, and they quickly move on. I devoted the entire previous chapter to the biology of love because I think the place of biology in this story is too important and complicated to pass over quickly. In fact, many of the most important philosophical questions about love arise precisely at the interface between love's social construction and its biology. At a minimum, we must understand the biology of love to understand what belongs on the social side and what doesn't.

But it's not surprising that biology typically fails to loom large in the thinking of social constructionists. When it comes to theorizing about the nature of a phenomenon—be it love or anything else—social constructionism is typically set in opposition to the biological approach. Consider a 1992 article by Williams Jankoviak and Edward Fischer titled "A Cross-Cultural Perspective on Romantic Love."[3] Jankoviak and Fischer point out that a majority of anthropologists and psychologists have previously assumed that romantic love is a social construct, but some "evolutionary-oriented" scientists (including Helen Fisher, whose work we discussed in chapter 1) have started to ask whether it might be a "human universal" centered on a "biological core." "This evolutionary perspective," they say, "suggests that romantic love arises from forces within the hominid brain that are independent of the socially constructed mind."

Jankoviak and Fischer then corral empirical evidence and analysis to make the case that romantic love is indeed a biological human universal and not a social construct. They analyzed data from 166 cultures, looking for evidence of the presence of romantic love. Although they failed to find such evidence in nineteen of the cultures they studied, they "believe[d] that these negative cases result[ed] from ethnographic oversight." Because they found romantic love to be present in the remaining 147 cultures, they concluded that it can be "muted, but never entirely repressed," by social factors.

However, we should question what exactly they were measuring. They define romantic love as "any intense attraction that involves the idealization of the other, within an erotic context, with the expectation of enduring for some time into the future." This makes it sound a lot like they were measuring a form of sexual infatuation. As a baseline, romantic love surely has to be a kind of love, but the Jankoviak-Fischer definition doesn't seem to require this.

Another pressing question is just what it would take for romantic love to be a human "universal." Jankoviak and Fischer examined cultures for whether romantic love is present in them at all. But Beall and Sternberg were looking at the ways romantic love varies across cultures. Love might be "universal" in one sense but not the other: even if it is always present, it could be substantially different in different cultures, and the latter kind of variation might still be evidence of social construction.

Jankoviak and Fischer's results are nevertheless interesting and suggestive: they indicate that something in the broad vicinity of romantic attraction transcends even extremes of cultural difference. Biology may yet be a bigger part of the puzzle than a simple social constructionism can account for.

By this point the picture is starting to look deeply complex. The complexity seems to involve a clash between social constructionism and the biological approach. And yet there is clearly wisdom on both sides. This tangle requires careful unpicking; we can give up any hope of a quick fix or an answer we can sum up in a platitude. Once again, I find myself starting to wonder what is real here.

What Is <u>Real</u>, Part II

While Beall and Sternberg's constructionism may not be the whole story, they are clearly right about the social significance of romantic love in many cultures. This is closely tied to love's social function: its role in structuring a society by providing contours for how intimate, loving relationships are supposed to be configured. It defines the tramlines, as it were, along which we expect our relationships—and our lives—to run. Beall and Sternberg put it this way: "Conceptions of love reflect cultural ideas about humanity."

Think of how Enlightenment love was taken to be under rational control, whereas Romantic thinkers treated love as uncontrollable and tumultuous. This parallels a shift in the dominant understandings of human nature, from fundamentally reasonable and rational (Enlightenment) to fundamentally passionate and untamed (Romantic). Different ways of socially constructing love "implicitly define what is appropriate and desirable in human relations," as Beall and Sternberg say. For example, conceptions that they describe as "Western"—wherein romantic love is construed as a suitable basis for marriage—predominate in individualistic societies organized around a nuclear family structure. By contrast, they associate the prevalence of arranged marriages with extended family structure and collectivist social attitudes.

As with Fisher's biological theory, I feel basically persuaded by the gist of Beall and Sternberg's social constructionism. But I am hesitant about it for two reasons. First, from a philosophical perspective, it can't be the whole story: biology is part of the puzzle. And second, I want to spell out the details of love's social construction in my own way.

Before I go into those details, though, let me highlight two common mistakes about social constructionism. These mistakes tend to crop up in discussions of the social construction of gender, race, and other things too, so they're well worth clearing up: just keeping these two points in mind will put you ahead of the game in most conversations about social constructionism.

The first mistake is to imagine that social constructs are a kind of fantasy or fiction. There is a temptation to say that anything socially constructed is "made up" and hence not "real." A 2015 *Globe and Mail* column by Margaret Wente contains multiple examples of this slip in quick succession: "Race and sex are more than social constructs. They also are facts. And you can't change the facts the way you change your shirt. . . . Gender, for example, is no longer viewed as an inescapable biological fact, but is really an arbitrary product of our belief systems. . . . Race, too, is often said to be a fiction. . . . Yet as a social construction, it is an awfully sturdy one."[4]

This sort of thing is common, but it is a serious error. Many social constructs are very real (and, incidentally, many are far from arbitrary). Just think of business corporations, universities, laws, political parties, birthday parties, or the country where you live. All of these things are created by social institutions, practices, and traditions. But they obviously don't belong to the realm of fiction, alongside Sherlock Holmes and unicorns. Laws are as much a part of real life as mountains and kittens. If we wrote two big lists of things that are real and things that aren't, Holmes and unicorns would go on the "not real" list, but laws would go with mountains and kittens on the "real" list. Socially constructed things are playing vital roles in your life right now if you live in a country with a government, use a currency, work for a business, or are the legal guardian of a child.

The second mistake is to imagine that social institutions, practices, or traditions that one finds abhorrent do not give rise to real social constructs. For example, if someone finds violence toward the innocent abhorrent and on that basis decides that any law prescribing or condoning such violence is not a real law, that person is making this second kind of mistake. Laws are just as real when they are unethical or misguided. There was a very real law against male homosexuality in England in the 1950s; among its very real effects was "chemical castration," to which the famous logician and philosopher Alan Turing was subjected. Immoral laws shape people's lives, and it takes real work to dismantle them. If they weren't real laws, they wouldn't be such a problem.

In an analogous way, a set of misguided social norms and traditions can give rise to a social construct of romantic love that needlessly and harmfully excludes same-sex love. This social construct is no less real on account of its being based in unethical practices. It still impacts people's lives, and it takes work to change a situation like this. So to sum up my two main points here: many social constructs are real, and some of them are really awful. If romantic love is indeed a social construct, that doesn't mean it isn't serious business or that it isn't seriously messed up.

K-I-S-S-I-N-G

Now for some of the details. Think how much information about love is packed into a playground rhyme:

> *[Name] and [name] sittin' in a tree*
> *K-I-S-S-I-N-G.*
> *First comes love, then comes marriage,*
> *then comes baby in a baby carriage.*

This rhyme teaches children what love is by teaching them what love does: it ingrains in their minds the idea of romantic love as occupying a place between physical affection on the one hand and marriage-plus-reproduction on the other. It also presents love as something that involves two people (there are only spaces for two names in the rhyme) and is typically hetero (usually one girl's name and one boy's name are used).

My theory about love's nature is ultimately a version of the old adage that "love is as love does."[5] And this one cute rhyme conveys such a lot of information about what love does. Love, the rhyme tells us, takes as input two people (of different genders) who are (physically) affectionate, and it outputs a nuclear family. Love is a nexus, connecting these important dots in social life. That is its function, its role.

In a society that values romantic love as its primary model for a "normal" life, powerful feelings of care and desire that one experiences for another person will tend to be focused toward the creation of a marriage-based, monogamous, lifelong, reproductive family unit with that person. Once formed, that nuclear unit can be locked in by providing social and legal benefits (such as tax breaks, social approbation, and hospital visiting rights) that incentivize staying together, while making the alternatives (separation and divorce) costly and complicated.

Romantic love has the function of structuring society into nuclear family units, harnessing the powerful forces of adult attraction, affection, and care to that end. It works so well that it becomes easy to forget that the default nuclear family is not the only way to structure social life. We could all live in larger communal groups. Or we could all live much more isolated lives. Or we could treat a wide range of social configurations as normal rather than seeing any one model as the "default." But we don't. We (literally) romanticize romantic love, and in so doing we hand it the power to structure society—to direct us into nuclear family units. That is the real power of love.

But is this a good thing or a bad thing? Well, it can be either. Often it's both. To explain why, let me say a bit more about what I think love is. First, romantic love is a kind of love. That much seems clear (although it is in danger of getting overlooked in some of the research). So what makes romantic love a kind of love? Well, it has features that any kind of love would have: it involves care, concern, trust, openness, and tenderness, for example.[6] I am not saying these things are social constructs; nor am I saying that all kinds of love are socially constructed. Social construction, in my view, comes into play in separating out certain kinds of love as "romantic." Romantic love's distinctive social function sets it apart from all other kinds of love.

This function is of the essence for understanding romantic love's social nature. Other kinds of love—such as the kind of love involved in a close friendship—do not have the same function: it is normally accepted that one may have as many friends as one cares to have, and there is no expectation that one will live with one's friends or have their children. If we do start experiencing very powerful feelings of care or desire for a friend, we are pressured to interpret this as falling in romantic love.

Of course, love's function doesn't always work out: love may go unrequited, face insuperable practical obstacles, fizzle, and so on. Love can fail to generate stable nuclear family units in all sorts of ways. But the very fact that these things get counted as "failures" goes to show what love is supposed to do.

And although love's function is important, that doesn't mean it's possible to count someone who just goes through the motions as being "in love"—that is, if they do all the kissing, marriage, nuclear family formation, reproduction, and so on, while feeling nothing. As I said up front, romantic love is a kind of love. Its distinctive social role is what makes it romantic, not what makes it love. Love isn't compatible with going through the motions and feeling nothing. And although it's not my main focus in this chapter, I do want to keep in mind that in addition to its social nature, romantic love has a biological profile that can help explain why it is associated with powerful feelings. (I will come back to this issue.)

I also don't mean to suggest that the social function of romantic love is unchanging or inevitable. On the contrary, social structures change, and the functional role of romantic love changes along with them. I am trying to capture what romantic love is—that is, what it does—around me here and now.

Supposing all this is on the right track, one of the most important consequences is that there is space for questioning and critiquing romantic love and specifically its role in structuring society. If we thought of romantic love as a universal, "natural," biological phenomenon, then social critique would seem unproductive and inappropriate. (We could bemoan the social consequences of headaches, but to cure them we need medicine, not marches.) But once we start to see how we are responsible for romantic love's social contours—how we create and sustain them through the cultural norms we accept and reinforce—everything changes. This way of understanding what love is suddenly throws open a whole range of possibilities for what love could be.

But what, now, has happened to the original case for thinking of love as biological? By this point it may be starting to look like things have gotten seriously tangled, and sooner or later we are going to have to choose. We'll either have to say romantic love is hardwired into our biology—a bundle of neurochemical responses that we've evolved to exhibit under certain circumstances—or that it is a social construct with a particular function in organizing society. Surely it can't be both. Our evolved neurochemistry is not a social construct. What gives?

I believe we can answer that question in a philosophically satisfying way. But before I explain how, I want to take a side step through some of the philosophical background. Philosophy has consistently both inspired and disappointed me in my efforts to understand love. So to put my work in context, let me take you on a whistle-stop tour through some of what philosophers have had to say about love over the years and where that leaves a philosopher of love these days.

3

Gems at the Garage Sale:
Philosophers on Love

And yet, to say the truth, reason and love keep little company together now-a-days; the more the pity that some honest neighbours will not make them friends.

—William Shakespeare, *A Midsummer Night's Dream*

Unlike Many Other Philosophers

When I first started studying what philosophers had to say about love, I have to admit I was disappointed. At its best, philosophical inquiry can be creative, original, exciting, and unsettling. It can reveal our hidden assumptions, forcing us to look them in the face and assess them for what they are worth. In real life, though, no discipline is perfect, and not everything done under the banner of "philosophy" is all that. Some of it is a frankly embarrassing catalogue of pompous people tripping over their own assumptions. Sadly, the philosophy of love is no exception.

But philosophy has inspired me too, so I want to start with some of the inspirations. Bertrand Russell is one philosopher who's inspired and influenced me in multiple ways. If you studied philosophy at university and came across Russell in that context, you might know him for his theory of definite descriptions (which tries to explain the inner logical workings of sentences that seem to be about nonexistent objects, like "The present King of France is bald"). Fascinating though this is, Russell's thinking about love and marriage had a far bigger impact on the world than his thinking about logic and language. Russell won a Nobel Prize for Literature in 1950 on the strength of his books for "a public of laymen," which, according to the award ceremony speech, contain a good deal of material that "excites protest"— and precisely this sets Russell apart. "Unlike many other philosophers, [Russell] regards this as one of the natural and urgent tasks of an author."[1]

One of his protested books was *Marriage and Morals*.[2] First published in 1929, this book now reads as considerably ahead of its time. Russell was a precursor of the contemporary "sex-positive" movement: he utterly rejected the idea that sex was shameful, sinful, or dirty. He called the repressive sexual mores of his own era a "morbid aberration," comparable to the prohibition of alcohol in the United States (i.e., producing outcomes of a lower quality but making them seem a lot more exciting than they really were). He thought we should be less prudish about pornography, scolded men for failing to make sex enjoyable for their female partners, helped campaign for the decriminalization of male homosexuality in the United Kingdom, and denounced the "blazing injustice" of treating sex workers with no respect. He stressed the importance of providing comprehensive information about sex—including birth control and sexual health—to young people. Perhaps most famously of all, he advocated for what in his time was known as "free love," foreshadowing contemporary notions of "open" and "monogamish" relationships.

Is Russell starting to sound a bit like Dan Savage to you? If so, that is a pretty fair comparison. But to give this some context, Russell published *Marriage and Morals* thirty-five years before Savage was even born. Still, Russell had what—in contemporary terms—we would call a huge platform, from which he could disseminate his progressive opinions widely, even when they utterly contravened prevailing social norms. Just as Dan Savage's platform rests on the success of a hugely popular advice column and podcast, Russell's sprang from his own prior achievements, albeit of a different kind: he traded on his outstanding early work in logic and the philosophy of mathematics, his scholarly reputation, and his affiliations with the University of Cambridge and the Royal Society. It's worth bearing in mind, too, that Russell's social class bolstered his ability to speak out on controversial topics: as a member of the British aristocracy, he was more audible than most of his contemporaries and better shielded from the consequences of voicing his views. Yet even with these advantages, Russell ran into serious trouble for thinking and speaking freely, eventually losing an academic job after scandalizing the world—or at least social conservatives in the

United States—with his attitudes toward love and sex. His work on these topics never secured a place in the established canon of academic philosophy, despite its impact on the world at large.

Bootleg Russell

Although love mattered deeply to Russell, over the years the very tradition of philosophy that he helped to launch has largely shied away from his style of publicly engaged critical thinking about things like love, sex, and relationships. As a student of philosophy at Cambridge, I was thoroughly put through my paces on Russell's philosophy of logic and language, and as a graduate student I delved into his philosophy of mathematics. But his views on love, marriage, and sex were never on the syllabus.

Naturally, this just makes them even more intriguing: Russell was not wrong about the psychological impact of attempts to keep something off people's radar. Discovering *Marriage and Morals* felt like discovering bootleg Russell: intoxicating if a bit dodgy. I was fascinated to read this work in which Russell is so compellingly at once both a philosopher and a human being.

It's not by chance that this book didn't make it onto my syllabus. Russell himself said that his work on love and other sociopolitical subjects was a separate business from his "philosophy." This distinction both reflected and reinforced conservative conceptions of what belongs in the academy. But whatever his classifications, Russell clearly considered his capacities for open-minded critical thinking relevant to the topic of love. And whatever he thought "philosophy" was, philosophy actually has a venerable tradition of engaged—sometimes unsettling—critical thought on hot sociopolitical topics, love included. Plato's *Republic* and *Symposium* are about how the state should operate and how people should practice love, and these works are at least as political and polemical as anything Russell ever wrote. Socrates was put to death for "corrupting the youth" with his unsettling conversations and for his "impiety" in questioning things one wasn't supposed to question. This kind of work has always been part of philosophy's remit. Twentieth-century efforts to redefine philosophy as a "pure" logico-scientific and apolitical pursuit were a temporary blip and ultimately a failure. My generation of philosophers is now coming to understand that academic philosophy was never apolitical (although pretending it was often led to a dangerous lack of awareness).

In any case, what Russell did in his philosophical work on love—as opposed to how he labeled it—is a source of inspiration to me. It was influential in my decision to write this book. But inspiration is complicated, and I don't want to give the impression that Russell is my hero. (He also expounded racist beliefs and displayed grossly dehumanizing attitudes toward disability.)

Despite the book's title, in *Marriage and Morals* romantic love is really the star of the show. Russell thought that sex should be treated as "experimentation with a view to love" and that marriage should be about the legal recognition and regulation of relationships based on love (its main purpose being to ensure the proper long-term care of the biological children born into loving hetero relationships). Note how, once again, romantic love is presented as playing a distinctive functional role in society: for

Russell, love is a nexus linking sexual experimentation on the one hand with stable reproductive nuclear family units on the other. We find in Russell more or less the same theory of love that the K-I-S-S-I-N-G rhyme conveys to children on the playground.

Russell's radical addition was that a love-based marriage need not be sexually or romantically monogamous. He proposed open marriages as an alternative, making the case that it is better to rein in jealousy than to rein in love. However, unlike his contemporary counterpart Dan Savage—who acknowledges that monogamy works for some while nonmonogamy works for others—Russell seemed to be proposing open marriage as the new norm for everyone.

So what did Russell think was so bad about monogamy? The answer lies in how he thought monogamous romantic love was connected to gender and power. He diagnosed the addition of monogamy into the social role of love and marriage as emanating from men's desire to secure reproductive control over women in order to create and maintain a patriarchal, family-based social order with property inheritance passing down the male line. (The idea of imposing sexual monogamy as a restriction on men, as Russell notes, is a more recent development.) Russell ultimately attributes patriarchy itself, with its attendant physical and mental "subjection" of women, to the discovery of how biological paternity works. He also emphasizes the role of religion in enforcing patriarchy, monogamy, and women's oppression (particularly Christianity, which Russell identifies as elevating fatherhood to a position of supreme importance).

As a consequence of all this, Russell says, it came to be seen as ideal for women to lack sexual desire altogether, since this made it much easier to control their reproductive potential. But this kind of situation could be sustained only if women were continually oppressed. Moreover, Russell regarded the imposition of monogamy on both sexes as a leveling down, not a solution: "If we may judge by appearances," he says, "women will tend to prefer a system allowing freedom to both sexes than one imposing upon men the restrictions which hitherto have been suffered only by women." Russell doesn't say exactly what "appearances" he is judging by here, but I assume he based this statement on his own experiences of interacting with women. In a similar vein, Russell wanted us to know that "women whose sexual life is uninhibited are as liable as men to [sexual] impulses," as far as he had been able to observe.

What Do We Want?

Eighty-five years on, these anecdotal hypotheses of Russell's are finally being taken seriously enough to be scientifically tested. The results are starting to make a cultural impact, evinced in the recent success of popular books like Christopher Ryan and Cacilda Jethá's *Sex at Dawn* and Daniel Bergner's *What Do Women Want*.[3]

To give an example, new empirical research by psychologists Andreas Baranowski and Heiko Hecht challenges the received wisdom that women don't want casual sex.[4] Back in the 1970s and 1980s, psychologists conducted a study in which an opposite-sex partner offered college students casual sex. All of the women declined, whereas three-quarters of the men accepted.[5] This could be interpreted as evidence that women are biologically driven to guard their eggs and virtue vigilantly and to tolerate sex only in return for marriage or money. At least, that is an easy conclusion to jump to under the influence of social messaging that hammers this idea home every day. But it's also possible that the women were scared: scared of social stigmatization or for their physical safety. In a famous passage published in 1982, Margaret Atwood explains how when she asked a male friend why men feel threatened by women, he said, "They're afraid women will laugh at them. . . . Undercut their world view." But when she asked some of her women students why women feel threatened by men, they told her, "They're afraid of being killed."[6]

In their study, Baranowski and Hecht reproduced the finding that women reject casual sex with an opposite-sex partner when propositioned in ordinary social situations. But they took their research a step further, testing what would happen if subjects received the same offer in an environment where they believed they would be safe from physical harm and social stigma. In this study, the huge gender disparity vanished. Women picked on average about three out of ten men they thought were available for casual sex, whereas men picked on average about four out of ten women. Twenty-nine of the thirty women in the study said they would like to have sex with at least one of the men on offer.

Recent studies also raise complex questions about whether women are biologically hardwired to prefer sexual monogamy. For example, psychologists Meredith Chivers and Amanda Timmers conducted research that found women to be genitally aroused by erotic stories about encounters with strangers as well as with long-term partners.[7]

Bertrand Russell may have foreshadowed some of these findings, but philosophizing about what women—or, for that matter, men—want in the absence of empirical data is a risky business. That said, this risky business has been going for a long time. Back in 1884, political philosopher Friedrich Engels published *The Origins of the Family, Private Property and the State*, in which he hypothesized that monogamy would arise "naturally" if only love, sex, and marriage could be separated from concerns about property and inheritance, because women and men would want monogamy under ideal conditions.[8] He claimed that "sex-love is by its nature exclusive" (although he noted that in his time only women had realized this exclusivity), and so he predicted, "Remove the economic considerations that now force women to submit to the customary disloyalty of men, and you will place women on an equal footing with men. All present experiences prove that this will tend much more strongly to make men truly monogamous, than to make women polyandrous." It's unclear exactly what counts as "all present experiences" here, though presumably Engels's own experiences are included.

Engels beat Russell to the idea that bourgeois monogamous marriage was designed to assure men of paternity and secure the inheritance of property by their biological male offspring. (Engels added that its other role was to ensure that women provided men with unpaid domestic labor.) But on the question of what women want, these two men had very different ideas, though both reported basing their ideas on "experience."

But what if Russell and Engels were both wrong? What if there is no single model of what women (or men) want? What if some of us "naturally" want monogamy and others don't? Perhaps

Russell and Engels simply knew different people, and that's why "experience" delivered such different verdicts to them. I'm just going to leave that idea there for now, but it will be important later.

While Russell was ahead of his time in some ways, in other ways he failed to see where things were heading. What, against the backdrop of 1920s Britain, must have sounded like a radical "free love" manifesto was not really as free or as radical as it might have been. While he recognized that there was nothing morally wrong with sex between two men, he still thought of romantic love, marriage, and child rearing as limited to hetero couples—in fact, he found this so obvious as to require no comment. Russell was radical for his time in defending the idea that premarital sex should be acceptable for women as well as for men and that marriage should not require sexual exclusivity. But for all he may have been sex-positive by Victorian standards, he still thought sex without love was of "little value." And he still ultimately presented extramarital sex and love as inevitable and forgivable rather than as things people might actively choose and prefer for their own sake.

It Must Be Love

I'm disturbed by, but haven't yet mentioned, another feature of Russell's philosophy of love. This one relates to a deep-seated assumption that is still widely shared, which means it's a bit trickier to bring to the surface. So I'm going to approach it in a roundabout way, via what philosophers call the "union view" of romantic love.

The union view says that romantic love consists in union with another person and/or a desire for such union. (You might recall that Robert Nozick put forward a version of this view.) Now, Russell himself doesn't explicitly say union is the defining characteristic of love, but he certainly thinks it is one of love's important features: he writes that love "breaks down the hard walls of the ego, producing a new being composed of two in one." He acknowledges the fear of losing one's own individuality in the process of becoming part of a "new being," but he calls this fear "foolish," since "individuality is not an end in itself," and the loss of separateness is actually required for a satisfying life. Love, for Russell, is "the best thing that life has to give."

This sentiment might sound sweet, even cute. But it's not. A word recently coined by philosopher Elizabeth Brake describes Russell's attitude here: amatonormativity.[9] This coinage derives from the Latin words *amare* (to love) and *norma* (a standard against which things are measured). Amatonormativity says that romantic love is the normal or ideal condition for a human life, so lives that don't include it are imperfect or abnormal. Russell's amatonormative attitude becomes especially pronounced when he says that those who haven't experienced mutual sexual love "cannot attain their full stature, and cannot feel towards the rest of the world that kind of generous warmth without which their social activities are pretty sure to be harmful." He says, "The resulting disappointment inclines them towards envy, oppression and cruelty."

This is a horrible—and untrue—thing to say. Many well-adjusted, happy, productive, and socially valuable people are single and haven't been in love; some by choice, others as it happens.

Some of them are parents. Some care for relatives or friends. Most are ordinary people going about their business. It is outrageous to write them all off as "disappointed," "envious," failing to "attain their full stature," and harmful to society. But this is the consequence of assuming that romantic love is required for a satisfying life. Like I said: not sweet and not cute.

Russell's amatonormativity gets even more alarming when you appreciate that it encompasses his heteronormativity too. When he calls love "the most fructifying of all human experiences," he means what he elsewhere calls "serious love between a man and a woman." In a similar spirit he also denigrates the childless, saying, "Sex relations which are serious cannot develop their best potential without children and a common life." (This dig hits me personally, as I have no kids and no current plans to acquire any.)

Russell held dismissive and belittling attitudes toward various deviations from what he regarded as the norm. While he was busy arguing for greater acceptance of his own particular deviations, he might have done a better job of noticing how he was recycling and reinforcing the exclusion of those who deviate in other ways.

Heroes and Humans

But I already said that Russell doesn't belong on a pedestal. Nor does any philosopher or, indeed, any human. Nevertheless, it's a sad fact that philosophy sometimes fosters a culture of hero worship around certain figures, whose pronouncements—however awful, unoriginal, or just plain boring—come to be treated as important by default. This is deleterious to great philosophy. Unfortunately, the philosophy of love is an arena in which this problem has really shown its true colors over the centuries. Its effects are bolstered and concealed by the pretense that philosophy is a purely apolitical and rational pursuit, in which approbation and canonization are accorded purely on the basis of "merit"— not status, class, gender, race, or anything else.

In fact, philosophy has a long history of treating the ideas of men as agenda setting, according women's work a secondary place—or no place at all—in its canon.[10] Let me tell you about a recent book titled *Love: A History* by philosopher Simon May.[11] In this book, May traces "two millennia of Western thought," as the cover promises. It's an impressive book from which there is much to be learned. But here's the thing: *Love: A History* includes ten chapters that focus on specific named thinkers. Most of these chapters are about one person, though a couple are about two. So all in all, twelve people get the honor of appearing in a chapter title. And without exception, all twelve are white men. They are, in fact, a selection of what we might call the "usual suspects": Plato, Aristotle, Lucretius, Ovid, Spinoza, Rousseau, Schlegel, Novalis, Schopenhauer, Nietzsche, Freud, and Proust. When the dust jacket advertises the book as an exploration of "the very diverse philosophers and writers who have dared to think differently about love," it prompts one to wonder what counts as "diversity" in philosophy.

Women thinkers do not get chapters of their own in May's *Love: A History*, but women appear as a topic of discussion. There is a chapter titled "Women as Ideals," and there is an index entry

for "women," which includes subentries like "as intellectual beings" and "as temptresses." (There is no index entry for "men," and
to my knowledge it has not often been up for discussion whether
men are "intellectual beings" or "tempters.") May's book reflects
a pattern that it did not create (but does help sustain). Understanding that pattern is important for understanding the history
of the philosophy of love. If we interpret it incautiously, we risk
coming away with the impression that the philosophy of love is
done *about* women rather than *by* them.

It is hard to know exactly what has been responsible for
the devaluation and exclusion of women's voices in philosophy,
though it is almost certainly a mix of factors. Recent research
suggests this stems in part from an ingrained association between "genius" or "brilliance" and maleness.[12] This association
may not be deliberate or conscious, but if you ask people just
to close their eyes and picture a "genius," they are liable to picture an Einstein, a Darwin, or a da Vinci. If at some level we
associate being a great philosopher with being a genius, and we
also associate being a genius with being a (white) man, it is not
surprising if women somehow just don't seem to strike us as
great philosophers.

I also wonder if the image of *analytic* philosophy, in particular, as a male activity may have had something to do with what
Russell—a founder of the analytic tradition—chose to classify as
"philosophy" among his own writings. Is it a coincidence that he
categorized *Marriage and Morals*—which discusses stereotypical
women's business like love, marriage, family, and gender—as not
being philosophy, reserving that label for his work on stereotypical men's business like logic, mathematics, and the mind?

Even now, some regard books like *Marriage and Morals* as off-limits for "real" philosophy. In my opinion, philosophy is not so limited; only its practitioners are. Philosophy itself has a lot of unrealized potential in this domain.

Laurels and Facepalms

The situation I'm describing has impacted our collective philosophical conversations. To see how, let's take a brief tour through some murky corners of the "canonical" philosophy of love. In *The Gay Science* Friedrich Nietzsche says that he "will never admit that we should speak of equal rights in the love of man and woman: there are no such equal rights."[13] He backs this up with the old chestnut that love is not the same for men as for women: "What woman understands by love is clear enough: complete surrender (not merely devotion) of soul and body, without any motive, without any reservation. . . . [H]er love is precisely a faith: woman has no other." He adds that a woman "wants to be taken and accepted as a possession" and draws a fairly explicit analogy between the "perfect" woman in love and a slave. (By contrast, Nietzsche thinks that when a man is in love, he wants devotion and surrender from a woman.)

This may all sound strange and horrifying, but it fits neatly into Nietzsche's broader thought. In *Beyond Good and Evil*, he speaks of woman's incomprehensibility and opines that her nature is more "natural" than man's. (These stereotypes are part of what Betty Friedan would later identify as the feminine mystique.) He also provides a long list of women's "causes for shame" and rants that "her great art is falsehood, her chief concern is appearance and beauty."[14] While reading such misogynistic statements from a philosopher who is still canonized today can be shocking, it is perhaps more comprehensible when one bears in mind that decisions about what belongs in philosophy's canon have proceeded hand in hand with the perception of philosophy as a primarily male enterprise.

With a sense of how Nietzsche views women and men, we can also look to his "definition" of love in another work, *Ecce Homo*: "Love, in its means, is war; in its foundation, it is the mortal hatred of the sexes."[15] This is an ancient cliché, and I mean "ancient" quite literally: the Roman poet Ovid discussed the same ideas nearly 2,000 years earlier. Today, they survive on the websites of men's rights activists. The idea that love is a sex war is not even the most bizarre claim about love in *Ecce Homo*. One contender for that title is Nietzsche's assertion that women all love him except for the infertile ones. If we stumbled upon these sentiments published unattributed on a random website, we would hardly take them for the thoughts of a great philosopher.

Like many canonized heroes, Nietzsche has apologists who will argue that he didn't mean what he appears to be saying in his misogynistic passages. Some say that he was really a feminist. If so, he was a feminist who was not very good at explaining feminism: he attributed calls for women's emancipation to the fact that defective (i.e., infertile) women hated other women who had turned out well (i.e., reproduced). But perhaps we mustn't take these things out of context? Perhaps they're ironic? One constantly hears such excuses for misogyny.

There is another possibility, though: Nietzsche thought he had figured out a way to send different audiences the different messages they wanted to receive. He might have been trying to invent the two-tone political dog whistle. Pssst, feminists: it's ironic, of course! Pssst, misogynists: finally, someone is brave enough to tell it like it is! But if such ambiguity is supposed to feed us what we want to hear, it leaves me completely unsatisfied. The philosophical tradition in which I was trained values clear and careful expression because in its absence one risks being seriously misinterpreted. And even before I knew there was such a thing as philosophy, I learned from my mother—who learned it from her grandmother—that there comes a point when you have to say what you mean and mean what you say.

Another canonized philosopher, Arthur Schopenhauer, wrote in *The World as Will and Representation* that however lofty or ethereal we might think it, love is really just "a more definitely determined, specialised, and . . . individualised sexual impulse."[16] In particular, it is a heterosexual impulse: "merely a question of every Hans finding his Grethe." (True to stereotype, only Hans has agency in the search process: Grethe, we must suppose, waits patiently to be found.)

Schopenhauer, like Nietzsche, sees himself puncturing a grand illusion. But he too is just recycling stereotypes, including this one: "By nature man is inclined to inconstancy in love, woman to constancy . . . for nature moves her, instinctively and without reflection, to retain the nourisher and protector of the future offspring." Conveniently, this means that "faithfulness in marriage is with the man artificial, with the woman it is natural, and thus adultery on the part of the woman is much less pardonable than on the part of the man." These assumptions about what is "natural" for women and men presage contemporary discussions about what we're biologically "designed" to do; in particular, Schopenhauer's emphasis on humanity's impulse and instinct for reproduction—a drive, so to speak—foreshadows the contemporary metaphysics of love put forward by Helen Fisher. In many respects, Schopenhauer was only a mouthpiece for social norms that long predated him and have long outlived him. His sexism is uncritical, and so is his heteronormativity.

The problem is that Nietzsche and Schopenhauer are "A-list" philosophers: celebrities of the philosophy world, considered "geniuses." Their thinking has shaped perceptions of romantic love, human nature, women, and philosophy itself. Nietzsche and Schopenhauer each get a chapter of their own in *Love: A History*.

Both, like Russell, were the beneficiaries of multiple forms of social privilege; they were white, male, and middle- or upper-class. But in a sense this put them in a position of philosophical disadvantage. One's privilege can make it harder to get critical insights into the things affected by that privilege, for the simple reason that the workings of privilege are usually far easier to notice and understand when you are not their beneficiary. Beneficiaries of privilege often are not even aware of its existence: they have never needed to be. To compound this problem, it can be deeply uncomfortable to regard one's favorable position within a social structure as due to privilege rather than solely one's own merits and efforts. So the beneficiaries of privilege can be strongly motivated to ignore it. If you are trying to figure out how romantic love works at a time when it is intimately bound up with sexism, heteronormativity, and other systematic oppressions, privilege is a philosophical hindrance.[17]

The upshot of all this is that in order to do great philosophy of love these days, we need to turn to more sources than just philosophy's canon. And within philosophy, we need to look beyond just the usual suspects. We need to clear a path through the tired old tropes that have been blasted on repeat for so long to seek out some of the more interesting, less trumpeted voices.

A Sense of What Matters

It's not all Nietzsches and Schopenhauers in the history of the philosophy of love. Simone de Beauvoir addressed romantic love as part of a wide-ranging philosophical investigation of gender, and she developed conceptual resources for understanding both love and gender that are of importance for philosophy today (up to and including this book). In her best-known work, *The Second Sex*, de Beauvoir was among the first to develop the idea of gender as a social construct, which she summarized in her famous statement that "one is not born, but rather becomes, woman."[18] She identified various traits that we associate with womanhood: fragility, unintelligence, and unsuitability for leadership, for example. And she discussed the treatment of women as "other": that is, defined by their relationships to men, or what differentiates them from men, rather than as full subjects in their own right. Then she made the case that having particular genitalia at birth does not naturally or biologically determine such things. Instead, they are imposed by the society around us as we grow up. For instance, if boys' education is taken much more seriously than girls', it is not surprising if women then strike us as being less intelligent. (This echoes a theme in earlier work by pioneering philosopher of gender Mary Wollstonecraft.)

De Beauvoir's views on romantic love are not rose tinted. In "The Woman in Love," a chapter of *The Second Sex*, she points out that Nietzsche's description of what love is like for women is actually not far off the mark when considered critically, as a description of love in a deeply problematic society (rather than the "natural" order). Romantic love, as de Beauvoir sees it, is damaging and dangerous to both women and men. It encourages women to seek their own annihilation through absorption into a man's life and identity—otherwise, they risk being seen as unwomanly. But this is devastating to all the things that de Beauvoir, as an existentialist, considers necessary for an "authentic" life, in particular the freedom to choose one's own path. Moreover, women in romantic love are taught to see their male partners as impossibly idealized, since otherwise their own annihilation would be too obviously irrational. But no man is impossibly ideal. The inevitable failure to live up to the prescribed manly role in patriarchal romantic love thus ultimately makes love deeply damaging for men as well. However, de Beauvoir includes one note of optimism: she says that one day, when women and men can approach each other as equals, love will become a source of life (rather than mortal peril).

Philosophers have put the idea of social construction to work in considering many topics besides gender. For example, Lucius Outlaw, Charles Mills, and others have argued that race is a social construct. In this book, when I discuss romantic love as a social construct, I owe much to the philosophers who developed and refined this conceptual resource for me to work with.[19]

We can also find fascinating—and sometimes even stereotype-defying—work on the philosophy of love in much older texts. Plato put love (of various kinds) at the center of his philosophy, and intriguingly he put a woman philosopher of love at the center of his most famous work on the topic, the *Symposium*. He has the character of Socrates credit a priestess called Diotima—possibly a fictionalized version of someone Plato knew—as the source for the most serious and original theory of love that appears in the work. Diotima's theory of love is complicated and strange to modern ears, but one of its interesting features is the idea that all humans are pregnant either in body or in soul, and love brings forth their offspring (be it children, art, or philosophy).

Back in the present, philosophers are still at work figuring out what love is. In her recent book *On Romantic Love*, philosopher Berit Brogaard has defended the view that romantic love is a kind of emotion.[20] This classic philosophical view of love faces many challenges (including Fisher's argument that love is a drive). Brogaard develops a version in which emotion of romantic love can be either rational or irrational, which she thinks is important because "rational love leads to happiness," but "irrational love does not."

Several other contemporary philosophers of love are also interested in the rationality and reasonableness of love, and I find this trend interesting. Psychologists Anne Beall and Robert Sternberg can help us contextualize it: remember their discussion of how the Enlightenment view of human nature as fundamentally rational corresponds to the idea that love is ideally rational too? The current tendency among philosophers of love to focus on love's rationality and reasons makes me wonder if there is some Enlightenment-like conception of human nature at work behind the scenes in philosophy today.

As for me, when considering the relationship between rationality and love, I am drawn to something Bertrand Russell once said in a television interview. He was asked what messages he would want to send to future generations, and one of the two he picked was "Love is wise, hatred is foolish." I think his choice of words here is significant. He didn't say love was "rational" or "reasonable"; he said it was "wise." Why might that have been?

Well, we can step back here and think about the word "philosophy," which originally derives from a Greek word for love (the prefix *philo-* is related to *philia*, meaning "friendly affection") and a Greek word for wisdom (*sophia*). I have found it helps to keep this definition in mind when navigating contemporary analytic philosophy, which typically puts rationality and reason—not wisdom—center stage. This phenomenon stretches beyond the philosophy of love and has been bound up with analytic philosophy's self-conception as a logical, scientific, and apolitical enterprise.

I am a fan of rationality and reason, and I think they can be elements of wisdom. But I don't think they are all of it. Insightfulness can also be an important part of wisdom. So can creativity, originality, and—a quality that's often overlooked—a sense of what matters. This last is particularly important for thinking about love, when everyone has something to say and one of the biggest challenges is curating a path through the mass of information and opinions. I certainly think there is a place for questions about individual rationality and reasonableness when it comes to understanding love. But—inspired by Beall and Sternberg, de Beauvoir, and others—I also think it is important to keep a bigger, societal picture in view.

Let me finish up with a recap of two morals from this chapter. First, philosophers are not immune to making awful pronouncements about anything and everything, love included. Just like the biology of love, the psychology of love, the sociology of love, and every other ongoing cultural conversation about love, the philosophy of love is often a messy bundle of uncritical assumptions and flashes of insight. I see myself rummaging around in it like a pile of clothes at a garage sale: I've found some gems in there but also a lot of stuff I have no use for. And even with the gems—Bertrand Russell especially—I feel like I'd need to take them home and give them a good wash before I'd be comfortable wearing them. Philosophy has powerful tools to offer anyone who wants to better understand the nature of love, but proceed with caution when reading what philosophers have to say about it. This applies equally to the book you are reading right now.

The second moral is that while I've found interesting gems, I have not found what I'm looking for. My own sense of what matters keeps insisting that the most urgent task facing a philosopher of love right now is to find a satisfying resolution to this book's central dilemma: How can love be both biological and a social construct? That work is still waiting. It's time to turn to it in earnest.

4

Love Is as Love Does: Love's Dual Nature

What ever dyes, was not mixt equally . . .
—John Donne, "The Good-Morrow"

Having It All

Biological and social theories of love both tug on my heartstrings. When I notice my heart beating faster at the thought of a loved one or feel the rush of adrenaline when we are together after an absence, I am drawn to the biological view. There's nothing socially constructed about this love that I'm experiencing: this is a natural phenomenon. If I want to understand what's happening to me, I need to understand what my brain and my body are doing. Advances in biological and psychological sciences are making it clearer and clearer that a human in love is just what

every other human is: an animal with a biology and a complicated evolutionary history. These features of ours are natural.
They are discoverable. If we do good enough science, we'll figure
them out.

Then again, when I get frustrated with the social norm of
universal monogamy and hearing about how being in two
relationships means I'm not "really" in love, it seems obvious that
romantic love is what we—collectively, socially—make of it. We
may have chosen to make it monogamous, but it doesn't have to
be that way. There's this package of traditions and expectations
that we've bundled together and labeled "romantic love," and it
gives our society a certain structure. But as soon as we know a
little history, sociology, or cultural anthropology, we see clearly
that this isn't the only way a society may organize itself.

This is enough to land me squarely in the dilemma set up in
my first two chapters. How can love be both biology and a social
construct, when biology is not a social construct? The dilemma
presents us with a series of choices, arranged roughly as follows.
(These things aren't perfectly aligned but broadly correlated.)
On the one hand, we could approach love as a natural phenomenon. We could start from the assumption that it is universal (or
nearly so) in our species. We could attempt to learn more about
it by studying individuals belonging to that species, deploying
the methods of natural science. On the other hand, we could
approach love as a social construct, starting from the assumption
that it is localized to specific cultural contexts. We could try to
learn more about it by studying societies, deploying the methods
of the humanities and social sciences.

It's tempting to try to have it both ways: to say that love is both biology and a social construct. In fact, quite a lot of theories of love initially sound like they're trying to do just that. But—disappointingly—on closer inspection it usually turns out that either they aren't saying this at all, or they never explain how it's possible. The desire to have it both ways is fairly common, but coming through with the goods is much more challenging.

One way of gesturing at the idea that romantic love is both biological and social is to say that society or culture shapes how love is expressed, while love itself is an underlying biological phenomenon.[1] This downplays the importance of the social side of love, however, relegating it to mere expression. It is a truism that culture shapes expression. The wisdom that I'm looking to preserve—that romantic love is a social construct—is not a truism (and it's not about expression). Another such gesture is to say that culture—art and literature, for example can be a source of clues about what love must be like.[2] But this, again, downgrades the role of culture to signposting: something that just provides us with pointers to where the real (biological) action is.

On the other hand there are those who gesture toward both the social and biological but ultimately opt for a social theory of love. One version of this strategy is to say that romantic love is a social invention, albeit one prompted by biology. In this kind of approach, the biology of love gets downgraded to a mere historical precursor.[3]

The third common strategy is simply to state that love is both biology and society without doing anything to resolve the appearance of contradiction this creates.[4]

Stand Back: I'm Going to Try Metaphysics!

There is still work to do. This is conceptual work: we need to reexamine our ways of thinking about love—about what is real and what isn't, what is natural and what isn't—in order to make sense of what looks like a contradictory situation. It is, in fact, just the kind of work metaphysicians do.[5]

I propose a new theory of romantic love. At its core is the idea that romantic love has a dual nature: it is *ancient biological machinery* embodying a *modern social role*. The real conceptual work, however, is to see how love's dual natures fit together. Here it helps to think of an actor playing a role in a TV show. As you're watching the show, you might notice various things about the character: his haughty behavior, perhaps, or his complicated relationships with the other characters. At the same time, you might notice various things about the actor: his smoldering eyes, as it might be, or his almost unsettling facial symmetry. There's nothing strange about the fact that in watching the show we notice features of the character as well as features of the actor. It would be strange, however, to ask which one we were really looking at, the character or the actor. As soon as we understand the relationship between actor and role, that seems like a silly question.

Romantic love is like this. Some of our ancient, evolved biological machinery—a collection of neural pathways and chemical responses—is currently playing the starring role of Romantic Love in a show called *Modern Society*. As we watch this show play out, we might notice various things about the social role (the "character," as it were): the way it structures a society into nuclear families, maybe, or its complicated relationship with gender. At the same time, we might notice various things about the biology (the "actor"): the involvement of dopamine, say, or the brain regions that are implicated.

The crucial point is that nothing determines that one of these aspects of love's nature is what love really is to the exclusion of the other. Of course, we could decide to use the phrase "romantic love" only to talk about the social role or only to talk about the biological machinery. But the current meaning of that phrase is vague and imprecise: it doesn't force either interpretation. The full story will be one about love's dual nature.

Love's biological machinery is something natural, which we discover rather than create, to be studied primarily by the natural sciences. It is something we would expect to be a human "universal" in the sense of being consistent across time and place, though we can still expect to see interpersonal variation, as with other aspects of our biology. It is something we can investigate by studying individuals, while acknowledging that it is also important to understand how we have evolved as a species.

Love's social role, on the other hand, is (at least partly) an artifact, which we create in the process of setting up a societal structure, to be studied primarily by the humanities and social sciences. And it is something we would expect to be localized to specific times and places, though we should anticipate influences and similarities across time and place, as with other aspects of culture. It is something we can investigate by studying societies, while acknowledging that it is also important to gather a diverse range of individual perspectives.

What does all this mean? Well, it means it is right to say that romantic love is a social construct. And it is also right to say that romantic love is a biological phenomenon. Most importantly, we're not contradicting ourselves in saying so, any more than we're contradicting ourselves when we point to our TV screen and say, "There's William Shatner!" then go on to say, "There's Captain Kirk!" What's on the screen? William Shatner embodying the role of Captain Kirk. What is love? Ancient biological machinery embodying a modern social role. Omit either half of the description, and you just aren't seeing the full picture.

Who's Running This Show?

Appreciating that love has a dual nature is just the beginning. We immediately need to ask a few crucial follow-up questions. The most important is, Which of love's features belong to its social nature, and which belong to biology? We know that the line "Beam us up, Scotty!" is part of the script for a character (Captain Kirk) but that the particular mouth we see on the screen speaking that line is the mouth of an actor (William Shatner). We understand how the interactions between the two can make for great television. We need to think about love the same way: to identify what is part of the social script, what is contributed by the biological actor, and how these things interact. Among other things, this is essential for understanding what kinds of control we have over the nature of love and what love could become in the future.

Let's think about the idea of control. In understanding that love has a partly social nature, we open the door to critical examination of the particular way romantic love currently structures social life. We acknowledge the possibility of real, substantive change. Feminists have critiqued the role of romantic love in, for example, creating and maintaining harmful gender norms, and queer theorists have critiqued its role in, for example, justifying homophobia. These efforts have resulted in real changes to the script: real changes to what love is (and what it does) at the social level.

When it comes to the biology of love, however, it's much less obvious that such control is possible. Our brain chemistry evolved long before contemporary social structures and may well outlast them. By appreciating the biological aspect of love, we can get a handle on what persists through social change. This is fascinating in its own right, but it too has practical implications in terms of what we can and cannot control. Sometimes knowing our own biology may reveal limitations on what kinds of change are feasible (at least until we can alter our biology). In other ways, the biology of love can provide motivations for change; I'll come back to this later in the book.

Unless we're careful, though, it will be all too easy to attribute things to biology that we actually have no evidence are biological. Humanity has a long and embarrassing history—that isn't over—of coming up with "biological" theories of x that have no grounding in reality or evidence but "feel right" because they gibe with the dominant ideology of the moment. Biological theories of race are used to justify slavery or mass incarceration. Biological theories of gender are used to justify rape or depriving women of education and property. History testifies that once we are ideologically invested in a status quo, we try very hard to prove—with biology—that it is the "natural" order of things.

This enables a dominant ideology to reinforce itself: prejudices and injustices appear immune to criticism or challenge if attributed to a biological or natural cause. For example, if we can convince ourselves that women are biologically different from men in ways that make them bad at mathematics and politics but good at child care and laundry, then we can justify a social structure in which women do all the (unpaid, repetitive) household labor: it is the "natural" state of things. Any attempt to change this situation is "going against nature," which will make everyone miserable and is doomed to failure because you can't change biology.

If we want to do the philosophy of love well, we ignore this history at our peril. Like gender and race, romantic love is an intense focus for values, political convictions, and emotions. This creates the perfect storm when it comes to attempting to discover the biological reality of love. We have already seen some ideology-driven accounts of how love "naturally" is. Recall, for example, Arthur Schopenhauer's thesis that love is all about "each Hans finding his Grethe" and how he insisted that monogamy was much more "unnatural" for men than for women.

To add one more recent example, clinical psychologist and couples therapist Sue Johnson claims in her book *Love Sense* that humans in general are naturally monogamous by biological design.[6] In arguing for this claim, she emphasizes the role of oxytocin in attachment and bonding, comparing us to prairie voles, who bond in couples, raise offspring with their mates, and also produce oxytocin that seems to play a significant role in that bonding process. However, prairie voles are not monogamous—at least not sexually. Johnson does not think this impacts her argument that humans are naturally monogamous, however. Her reasoning on this point is not clear,[7] which suggests possible interference from an ideological desire to reinforce the current cultural norm of monogamy.

The interference between insufficiently examined ideology and what we feel inclined to call "natural" or "biological" often runs very deep and makes itself invisible from the inside. This does not mean we should despair of the biology of love. It just means we must try to approach it with awareness of the risks and with a questioning, philosophical mind-set.

Nothing Artificial Added

To see what I mean, let's return to Helen Fisher's biological theory of love.[8] Fisher says romantic love emerged during our evolutionary history "to drive men and women to focus their mating attention on a preferred individual," and so "the brain circuitry for male-female attachment developed to enable our ancestors to live with this mate at least long enough to rear a single child through infancy together." Right away in these passages, we see a strong association between romantic love and reproduction. (Again, the theory of love on offer is not far from that found in the K-I-S-S-I-N-G rhyme.) There is also an immediate association between love and hetero coupling, conveyed in the unquestioned deployment of phrases like "men and women" and "male-female attachment."

Fisher goes on to associate the evolution of romantic love with specific reproductive gender roles. She says the arrival of bipedalism in our evolutionary ancestors "caused a problem for females: they became obliged to carry their babies in their arms instead of on their backs." And then these females "began to need mates to help feed and protect them—at least while they carried and nursed a child." Here the evolutionary origins of love get tied to the idea that females have a principal role in child rearing, and this renders them needy and dependent on males. Fisher presents the nuclear family—and hence the evolution of romantic love's brain circuitry—as evolution's solution to this female neediness. Correspondingly, the "male-female attachment" she identifies as the sequel to "romantic love" normally lasts approximately four years—just long enough to get a child through infancy.

Fisher also strongly associates romantic love with monogamy, which in turn gets linked back to female neediness. She says that with the arrival of bipedalism, pair-bonding became "essential" for our female ancestors. By contrast it only became "practical" for males. (The relevant practicalities are gestured at in asides like "How could a male protect and provide for a harem of females?" But I'm not sure what this kind of rhetorical question is supposed to establish, since in many species—humans included—this model has often been realized.)

In short, Fisher's whole account of the evolutionary origin of love is infused with norms around gender, reproduction, heterosexuality, and monogamy. All these norms happen to be the ones that are familiar from our own contemporary cultural setting. But what, really, is the biological evidence that female neediness is part of the natural order of things and the true evolutionary basis for romantic love? Fisher pictures a bipedal hominid who must carry a baby in her arms, imagines her being unable to thrive without relying on a male provider, and proceeds from there. But the "naturalness" of this picture may owe much to the social conditions in which we now find ourselves. After centuries of preventing women from owning property, being educated, working outside the home, and so on, it may well seem "natural" to think of women as needy and dependent: we are conditioned to see women as only suited to full-time child care while a man takes care of business. We see this pattern wherever we look, whether we're doing big things like electing officials or appointing CEOs or small things like deciding whom to hold the door open for in a corridor. And we'll see it when we are doing science.

As a philosopher, I have come to think that the biology and evolution of love are important for understanding what love is. That's why I think it's important to get them right. This means we have to go by what the evidence actually shows rather than by what feels "natural." Fisher's hypotheses may sound "natural," but they raise a lot of questions in my mind.

For example, Fisher estimates that bipedalism began among our ancestors around 3.5 million years ago, and she proposes that something recognizable as romantic love evolved between 1.8 and 1 million years ago, following the advent of language, which led to protracted childhood and hence—as she sees things—the need for a longer-term partner. But if over 1 million years passed between the arrival of bipedalism and the evolution of love, then there must have been other solutions to the problem of having one's hands full of babies that worked well enough to keep hominid evolution going for over 1 million years. What about extended infancy meant that we couldn't extend those solutions? And if bipedalism posed such a problem for female ancestors specifically, how come we didn't end up with male-only bipedalism? Why doesn't the development of universal bipedalism better support the speculation that child care was already a cooperative enterprise?

Moreover, if bipedalism was making life difficult for mothers carrying children in their arms for an extended period, would evolving a whole new fundamental biological drive have been a more efficient solution than the invention of a simple technology, such as the baby sling? In fact, drawing on a variety of research in his recent book *The Artificial Ape*, archaeologist Timothy Taylor places the invention of the baby sling earlier than 1.8 million years ago.[9] If he is right, then by the time Fisher says romantic love was evolving (1.8 to 1 million years ago), the problem of bipedal mothers having to carry babies in their arms instead of on their backs could already have been solved.

Even setting aside technology, evolving a whole new fundamental biological drive would be a pretty extreme solution to a problem that could be solved in simpler ways, such as through cooperative social child-rearing in nurseries. How often does evolution take a sledgehammer approach to a problem when efficient alternatives are available?

The Standard Model Comes as Standard

My guess is that the true story of love's evolution will turn out to be a lot more complicated than bipedal mothers having their hands full. One possibility is that adult cooperation is beneficial to our species, and for this reason we evolved a whole suite of brain mechanisms that promote social bonding through the formation of cooperative groups that include—but are not limited to—nuclear family units. The biological machinery of romantic love can then be understood as part of a complex system of overlapping mechanisms that evolved for the promotion of social bonding and cooperation in various configurations. This would deliver a better explanation of what really happens, as it would explain the coexistence of both "traditional" nuclear families and various other models. It wouldn't require us to think of romantic love as a sledgehammer evolutionary response to a single problem (and, what's more, one readily solvable by other means): romantic love would instead emerge as part of a larger cooperative evolutionary strategy.

By contrast, what I call a "standard model" approach guides Fisher's philosophical work on the nature of love. This is the idea that one way of doing things is "standard," and all others are deviations. For Fisher, the "standard model" is a hetero nuclear family model, complete with the reproductive gender roles and monogamous norms familiar from our contemporary cultural context. I've already unpacked the reproductive gender roles a little; let's now turn to the issue of monogamy.

Let's agree that as we evolved and infancy began to occupy a longer period, solo parenting would have become very challenging. The question is, Why assume that monogamous coupling of the kind most familiar to us is the default solution to that problem? Many societies have arranged child care in other ways. Some, for example, form polygamous family units. (This has typically been patriarchal polygamy: one man with many wives, and not vice versa. But bear in mind that most monogamous societies have practiced patriarchal monogamy, where women are controlled by their husbands.) Fisher says polygamy is a "secondary strategy" for human social organization, but it is controversial among anthropologists whether this is so. Some believe polygamy is the primary human strategy. There is also a case to be made that a third strategy—namely, a collective social approach—can be a better solution to the challenges of child rearing in a state of nature than either monogamous or polygamous family units, and that this collective approach may have been a "primary" strategy in our evolutionary past.[10] There have also been polyandrous societies, where women have multiple male partners. These are rarer, but recent research has found that they are not as rare as previously thought, and they occur worldwide. (Intriguingly, polyandry does not generally give rise to a gender-flipped patriarchy; it is more common in egalitarian societies.)[11]

Child rearing is hard. It's a small step to conclude that it's best accomplished through cooperation, which we already know humans are good at. It's not obvious, however, why we should think there is a single "standard model" for how humans will cooperate to raise children. Even less obvious is that the standard model would just happen to be the one that is culturally dominant around here these days, as Fisher seems to think. But rejecting Fisher's standard model doesn't mean we should conclude that some other model is standard. In *Sex at Dawn*, Christopher Ryan and Cacilda Jethá say, "The amoral agencies of evolution have created in us a species with a secret it just can't keep. *Homo sapiens* evolved to be shamelessly, undeniably, inescapably sexual."[12] They go on to suggest that monogamy is a struggle because it goes against our nature.

Here we're being offered another one-size-fits-all picture of human "nature," just a different one. It's almost as if Fisher were claiming that blue is the natural eye color for humans, and then Ryan and Jethá, noting that a lot of humans have green eyes, were countering that green is the natural eye color for humans. For some people, monogamy really doesn't seem to be a terrible struggle. They say it feels perfectly "natural" and delightful and right.

In new work, psychologists Rafael Wlodarski, John Manning, and Robin Dunbar have defended the idea that there are two different "phenotypes" when it comes to "mating strategy" in humans: the monogamous type and the promiscuous type. They construct a case that both men and women are split between the two types, with 57 percent of men preferring promiscuity, compared to 43 percent of women. They presented this work in a 2015 paper titled "Stay or Stray? Evidence for Alternative Mating Strategy Phenotypes in Both Men and Women."[13] But as the title suggests, the paper compares only two models of relationship preference: long-term monogamous bonding on the one hand and short-term promiscuous bonding on the other. People with a preference for lifelong nonmonogamous bonds are somehow not on the radar. Nor are people with a preference for short-term serial monogamy. In fact the authors collapse the whole idea that there is a difference between number and duration of relationships, leading them to make claims like, "Humans actually consist of a mix of short-term (promiscuous) and long-term (monogamous) mating phenotypes," as if "long-term" and "monogamous" were synonyms. To me, as a polyamorous reader in two long-term relationships, this just sounds like a conceptual confusion.

It's tempting to seek simple models that we can easily understand, but the realities of romantic love aren't simple. Oversimplifying a complex situation is not good science, and it's not good philosophy either. I have yet to see convincing evidence that a single standard model for human relationships is hardwired into our biology. Positing two types is a step in the right direction, but a very small one. As a species, modern humans are a romantically diverse bunch. What "comes naturally" to us varies: our infinite variety cannot be reduced to one or two standard models.

To the Exclusion of All Others

We've seen how a biological theory of romantic love can be deployed to connect love with specific gender roles and with monogamy. It can also be used to connect gender and monogamy with each other. For example, Fisher thinks that female neediness is the reason romantic love evolved and thus ultimately is what caused our ancestors to become monogamous. Nowadays, we are strongly socially conditioned to see monogamy as a thing that women desperately want and men grudgingly agree to. But what evidence is there, really, for the claim that women want monogamy?

Some contemporary research suggests the opposite: that women can struggle with monogamy at least as much as men do. Hetero women are apparently much more likely than hetero men to experience a loss of sexual desire in long-term monogamous partnerships. Psychologist Dietrich Klusmann investigated survey data from 2,500 participants and found that men and women reported equal lust for each other at the beginning of a relationship. However, as the relationship progressed, "a marked decline in sexual motivation occurred in women but not in men."[14] Other research casts into doubt the assumption that female sexuality is typically directed toward established intimacy. When psychologists Meredith Chivers and Amanda Timmers found that hetero women were often genitally aroused by erotic stories about encounters with either their long-term partners or male strangers, they also observed that erotic stories about the subjects' friends, despite all the established intimacy, did not elicit comparable levels of genital arousal.[15]

The methodological question of where to look for evidence of women's supposed "natural" preference is important. Strong social pressure to have (and express) preferences for monogamy creates conditions under which it is complicated to find out what women "naturally" prefer: simply asking what they want is prone to elicit the conditioned answer. We need a subtler approach: a search for clues. By measuring things like the drop-off in women's desire for long-term monogamous partners or their arousal by erotic stories about strangers, we can gather indirect evidence that may point to a rather different pattern of "natural" preferences behind the social conditioning.

We must also confront another problem with Fisher's standard model approach at this point. Just as we can question the assumption that romantic love is grounded in women's natural need for monogamy, we can question the assumption that romantic love is naturally geared to heterosexual reproduction. Fisher's mentions of same-sex romantic love in *Why We Love* are minimal and rather give the impression of being afterthoughts.[16] Indeed, given her standard model, Fisher has to treat same-sex love as a sort of deviation from the species norm, requiring an explanation at the level of individual developmental difference. She says, for example, that "gays and lesbians in all cultures also feel romantic passion. . . . During development in the womb or during childhood they developed a different focus for their passion." Same-sex love, in Fisher's picture, looks like an individual misfiring of machinery that evolved in our species for the purpose of heterosexual reproduction.

But same-sex love only calls out for explanation in terms of individual deviation if hetero reproductive coupling is built into the "standard model" to begin with. Given that we are strongly socially conditioned to expect romantic love to be hetero by default, we should be wary of assuming that biology made it so. We need to see the evidence. Once again, however, when we look at what we really know about biology and evolution, alternative explanations are readily available. Suppose romantic love evolved to promote intense—often sexually cemented—bonding between individuals leading to cooperation in a range of activities (including child rearing, among other important things). This gives us a more inclusive theory out of the box. If we didn't set out by assuming that love was originally all about "male-female" reproductive coupling, then we wouldn't later need to backtrack to try to accommodate queer love as some kind of deviation.

The scientific method exhorts us to seek evidence for our hypotheses rather than trusting hunches. This is nowhere more important than in the science of romantic love, which is politically loaded, hugely important socially, and intimately connected with our deepest ideas about human nature, gender, child rearing, and what makes for a good life. This is exactly the sort of area where we are terrible at having accurate hunches, but our terrible hunches keep being presented to us as objective science.

The Composite Image

Our hunches about love don't appear out of nowhere. We have been provided with a theory of what love is since before we can remember. Think back to the K-I-S-S-I-N-G rhyme. Something as simple and apparently innocent as that rhyme packs in a lot of information about what love is (and what it does). The rhyme serves to create an image of love—equivalent in essentials to Fisher's standard model—in the minds of children and to sustain this image as it gets passed down through generations.

And a huge range of other cultural products contribute to the same end: everything from high art (think of the two figures in Klimt's *The Kiss* and how much information the representation of their gendered bodies conveys) and literature (*Romeo and Juliet* is the ultimate classic heteroromantic tragedy) to religion (we could spend years unpacking the Adam and Eve story and its influence on romantic gender roles) and popular rom coms (*When Harry Met Sally*, not *When Harry Met Barry*, and certainly not *When Harry Met Barry and Sally*). Then there are all the Valentine's Day shop window displays, the relationship advice columns, the engagement ring ads, and the endless unsolicited information on "what women want" and "how to keep your man." It goes on and on. The character Kilgrave in the TV series *Jessica Jones* is not too far off the mark when he says, "I am new to love, but I do know what it looks like. I do watch television!"[17]

All these representations of romantic love add up to a composite image of what romantic love is like. I use the metaphor of a composite image to invoke the way that, when thousands of individual representations are overlaid, patterns or contours will gradually emerge. Imagine building a composite image of a person by overlaying a thousand photographs of different people who all share a similar chin shape but have different hairstyles. In the composite image, the contours of the chin will emerge as a clear feature, but the hair area becomes a fuzzy mess.

We need to look for the emergent contours in the composite image of romantic love: the features that come through clearly when we overlay all those representations that pervade our culture. One of these contours is the way romantic love functions to organize a society. It serves to harness—we might even say tame—a bundle of powerful (potentially disruptive) feelings and desires, channeling them into a safe, stable, nuclear family structure. Love's connections to sex, marriage, and reproduction are all related to this. And while romantic love emerges as something that allows individuals to exercise choice in selecting a partner, it's important to see how and why that choice is constrained.[18] It is part of romantic love's role to regulate sexuality and intense bonding by encouraging its development within just one structure—the permanent, heterosexual, monogamous couple (the kind of unit that heads up a "traditional" nuclear family)—while discouraging all other formations. Often there are other restrictions in play as well (based on race and class, among other things). The privileged formation is the one favored with the fullest and easiest access to social and legal benefits, such as marriage; the one that we must choose to minimize the risk of potentially devastating social stigma and rejection; and the one that is most widely and openly represented and celebrated across all forms of art, culture, and social life.

My point here is not just that this formation is being valued and promoted at the expense of others. It is,[19] but, more relevantly, all this representation and celebration of one particular formation are contributing to making romantic love what it is. This is the mechanism by which we collectively, as a society, create and sustain the strong contours that emerge in our composite image of romantic love. The image changes over time, and it is to a large extent under our collective control. But it shapes and defines what love is (and what it does) at the social level, providing us with a script that we are supposed to follow.

A Little Biology Goes a Long Way

Many of the features Fisher attributes to love's biology may indeed turn out to be part of the story of what love is—but more plausibly attributed to love's social script. Fisher wouldn't be the first—and won't be the last—to build more into a biological theory than really belongs there. There is no compelling evidence that all of our current nuclear norms for monogamous hetero reproduction have been programmed into love by biological design, but these norms *are* deeply ingrained elements of the social script for romantic love. They are among the strong contours that emerge in the composite image. That doesn't make them any less real, but it is nevertheless an important difference from a metaphysical and practical perspective.

I am basically persuaded by a subset of Fisher's biological theory of love: the parts where I can see robust connections to the evidence. Let me recap what these are and explain why they are so important. First, I am convinced by Fisher's evidence that romantic love often involves particular brain regions and chemicals. This helps us understand the physical similarities between romantic love and other things. (Oxytocin, for example, is involved in both romantic love and parental bonding; dopamine is involved in both romantic love and the reward system more generally.) Thinking of love in this way can also serve to remind us that, like all aspects of human biology, the biology of love varies from person to person.

Second, I agree with Fisher that the biological mechanisms involved in romantic love evolved over millions of years. We don't have to accept Fisher's specific explanations of why they evolved in order to appreciate that they did. This is important because it means the biology of love was emerging under very different conditions from those in which we now live, which is exactly why we should be wary of projecting elements of contemporary society onto biology.

Knowing all this is important because knowledge is power. Uncovering the biology of love is a step in dismantling the romantic mystique: the disempowering idea that love is an incomprehensible or magical thing we should not think too much about. Let's not forget that it took many years of serious scientific research to convince (most) people that there is no biologically superior race or gender. Getting a proper grip on the biology of love may help us unravel the idea that there is one biologically superior way to love.

But romantic love has a social function in addition to its biological profile: to take as input the attraction and affection that arises between adults and produce as output something resembling the nucleus of a nuclear family. This is the respect in which love is like an actor playing a character: there's the social role, and then there's the biological machinery playing the role. The work of Fisher and other biological scientists is important, but it only speaks to half of this story.

Now, it's not a total coincidence that certain actors get picked to play certain roles. Actors have features that make them a great casting choice for one part and a bad fit for another. Similarly, it is not a total coincidence that certain biological states in us play the social role of romantic love. But just as some casting decisions are better than others, so there can be a mismatch between love's biology and the social role it's expected to play. For one thing, society changes very rapidly compared to biology; what may once have been a good casting choice can quickly become a bad one.

We need to be able to explore these questions about the interactions between biology and society without pressure to choose one or the other as love's "real" nature. On the contrary, we must reconcile the insights and wisdom contained in both biological and social theories of love. We must apply social critiques to biological theories and vice versa without declaring either half of the equation intellectually bankrupt. And throughout this process we have to accommodate variety: at the biological level, at the social level, and in the interactions between the two.

I custom-designed my theory of romantic love to create a space for all of this. We can no longer make do with half a theory—not if we have set our sights on the big picture: love in all its incredible diversity. And not if we want to understand not only what love is but what it could be.

Rebel Without an Answer

If I know anything about romantic love by now, it's that it's not a one-size-fits-all phenomenon. Still, I'm left with a question: Does it fit me? Is the love I feel for my partners "romantic"?

My answer is—predictably—twofold: yes and maybe. The yes is for the biological aspect. I'm pretty confident my biology looks the way the biology of romantic love is supposed to look. Now to be fair, I haven't scanned my brain to check exactly what's up in there. However, I can report that it really feels like the dopamine, the oxytocin, and so on are doing their thing. I've been in monogamous love before, and it felt very similar. So I'm going to go ahead and say the biology is happening. The actor is on set.

As for whether it's playing the right social role to count as romantic love in my time and place, that's where I get the maybe. I'm not sure. It's not ruled out: my composite-image theory of the social construction of romantic love allows that not all of the "normal" features have to be present in every case. (Many couples count as in love who are of the same gender, have no plans to get married or have children, or in other ways don't fully conform to the script given to us by the composite image.) But monogamy may still be too close to being a core norm, here and now, for my situation to be clear-cut. As one indicator of this, in *On Romantic Love* Berit Brogaard classifies nonmonogamous relationships as an "in between case" of love, along with situations where someone is "just not that into you."[20] Perhaps monogamy is still so firmly built into the script that my biological actor doesn't count as playing the Romantic Love role in the *Modern Society* show.

But what do I care about modern society? Can't I just be a carefree rebel? Well, no. Maybe I can be a rebel, but I can't be a carefree one. In the society I inhabit, it's impossible to avoid the psychological impact of amatonormativity—that idea that if you're not in romantic love, or at least looking for it, then you're doing life wrong. While I don't agree with that on an intellectual level, the internalized attitude is hard to dislodge. The assumption is so prevalent among almost everyone I interact with that it's impossible to ignore, regardless of whether I personally agree. In the same vein, I can't just stop caring about monogamy norms because too many other people care about them. And last but not least, it's impossible for me to stop caring about whether my situation counts as a genuine case of romantic love because I know that its being recognized as such could be a powerful way of convincing people to take my relationships seriously.

So I'm sad about the maybe. But while my philosophizing isn't giving me the answer I initially wanted, it's giving me much more than that. It's giving me glimpses into what the real questions are and why they matter. Philosophy, once again, hasn't let me take the easy way out—and I appreciate it even more than I would have appreciated getting the answer I hoped for.

There is good news in the mix. Romantic love has the potential to be a far more inclusive phenomenon than normally assumed. Based on my thinking so far, I am coming to understand just how much capacity love has to change. Love's social role, at least, is quite malleable. Perhaps love's biology is too: the science is advancing to the point where such things are not unrealistic. Whatever I might find unsatisfying about love right now, I don't have to assume it will be that way forever. And that is a hopeful thought.

With this hope in mind, over the next few chapters I'll take a look at some of the ways romantic love has changed over the years and what kinds of change are still needed.

Under Construction:
Love's Changing Role

For stony limits cannot hold love out,
And what love can do, that dares love attempt.

—William Shakespeare, *Romeo and Juliet*

Which Kind of Stupid Are We?

Once we have a grasp of love's dual nature, we can rethink the whole idea that biological and social theories of love are in competition with each other.

Where did that sense of rivalry come from? Perhaps it's just that people love to sort themselves into binary categories: "Liberal" or "conservative"? "Male" or "female"? "Gay" or "straight"? We do it even when the binaries obviously don't make much sense: "cat person" or "dog person"? This phenomenon has recently manifested in the form of coffee shop tip jars that come in pairs, offering customers a quick hit of binary choice: "Sun" or "rain"? "Chocolate" or "vanilla"? The mechanisms that prompt us to do this in all areas of life have probably also helped inculcate the idea that we have to choose "Love is biology" or "Love is society."[1]

The thing is, anytime we make such a choice—especially about something important—it's easy to begin to feel like part of an in-group, with those who make the other choice forming an out-group. This encumbers us with a temptation to demonstrate, to ourselves and everyone else, that our in-group is superior and the out-group is inferior. In fact, we can quickly become unreasonably resistant to any evidence to the contrary.[2]

I have no objection to leveraging this element of our psychology to secure tips for baristas, but I do worry when it seems to be hampering our efforts to understand a complex world. The appearance of competition between biological and social understandings of love weakens both enterprises. In efforts to prove the out-group is inferior, social theorists of love can be dismissed as "unscientific" and "uninformed," while biological theorists can be labeled "unsophisticated" or "uncritical." Instead of learning from the insights of whichever group isn't our own, we simply write each other off as one or another kind of stupid.

We must resist this temptation. We stand to learn far more about love if we do, especially when it comes to understanding how and why love changes over time. Appreciating that process of change requires appreciating how love's biological nature and its social role fit together and what happens when they pull apart.

Aliens Versus Nineteenth-Century Lesbians

Imagine that, on another planet, there is an alien society very much like contemporary North American society. It's replete with alien rom coms, alien weddings, alien genders (associated with distinct reproductive roles like ours), caring alien relationships, monogamous alien pair-bonding for life as a cultural norm, and so on. In other words, imagine an alien culture that's constructed a social role for romantic love exactly like the one we have here and now. But suppose the biological machinery that makes up these aliens is completely different from ours. Instead of dopamine and oxytocin, the aliens might have no chemicals in their brains at all. Perhaps their heads are filled with a system of levers and pulleys. Or perhaps they don't even have heads.

The question is whether these aliens are capable of falling in love or not. If love is something in our biology, then we ought to say these aliens don't fall in love: they aren't made of the right biological stuff. Maybe they fall in something that looks like love, but to say they literally fall in love would be a bit like saying they have "heart attacks" just because they sometimes fall down clutching the places where their hearts would be if they had hearts (which they don't). No hearts, no heart attacks. No brain chemistry, no romantic love. So says the biological theory.

On the other hand, if love is a social construct, we should say the aliens do fall in love: they are doing everything right. They meet "the one," care very deeply for that one, form a bond, build a life, get alien married, raise alien spawn together, and so on. Just as different actors can play Hamlet in different productions, different kinds of biological machinery can play the romantic love role in different creatures. Or so says the social constructionist theory.

But instead of choosing between biology and society, I am saying that romantic love is ancient biological machinery embodying a modern social role. This gives us a slightly more complicated answer to the question of whether our aliens really fall in love. The answer is yes and no: these aliens fall in love at the social level but not at the biological level. For the dual-nature theorist, asking if the aliens fall in love is a bit like looking at two different actors playing Hamlet and asking if they're "the same guy." Here too the answer is yes and no: same character, different actor.

What if we took things in the other direction, keeping the biology the same but changing the social role? What if someone was in just the right kind of biological state to count as being in love but was prevented from participating in the social role of romantic love because the role excluded certain people? For this scenario, we don't need to reach for science fiction. Consider, for example, the situation of a lesbian couple in late-nineteenth-century England. Suppose they are in love biologically speaking: the parts of their brains associated with romantic love are active, and they are under the influence of oxytocin, dopamine, and so on.[3] But inflexible heteronormative restrictions on the social role of romantic love prevent these biological states from doing what they would otherwise do: they prevent the women from marrying, from expressing affection (except perhaps clandestinely), from parenting together, or from forming a nuclear family. Social norms severely curtail their ability to engage in any of the kinds of bonding associated with romantic love.

Anne Beall and Robert Sternberg—the psychologists who defend a social constructionist theory of love—mention this kind of case as an example of how love changes along with the culture of which it is a part. They note that some women in the late nineteenth and early twentieth centuries experienced, and described in their writings, emotionally intense relationships with their female friends, which included physical elements like kisses and caresses. However, they did not classify these as experiences of being in love. At that time the social role of romantic love simply did not allow for same-sex cases. It wasn't even up for discussion; romantic love was treated as being obviously and definitively "love between the sexes."

The social role of romantic love in UK society has since expanded to create room for the inclusion of lesbian romantic love. Since 2014, women in England have been able to marry other women if they choose. While discrimination persists, this represents a huge cultural shift in the social role of love over a couple hundred years.

Jailbreak My Heart

Knowing a little history teaches us that the social role of love changes over time. It takes more work to understand why and how.

When describing nineteenth-century lesbians from our contemporary perspective, we may want to say, "They were in love," because they met all the conditions from our point of view: they were in a state perfectly suited to play the social role of love as it exists here and now. That state just couldn't play the social role of love as it was constructed back then, with its built-in heteronormativity. Since the nineteenth century there has not been a biological change to the way queer people work; society changed, and the social role of love changed within it. Considering nineteenth-century lesbians makes clear (in a way that considering hypothetical aliens doesn't) what is at stake in this process of change. It reveals that we have choices and responsibilities. We can construct love's social role in ways that tend toward exclusion, repression, and oppression or toward inclusion, expression, and equality.

Social constraints can be powerful, but love's biology is powerful too. No amount of determination to construct a social role for love that excluded queer people managed to shut down the biological machinery of queer love. Over time, the biology won out: the social role expanded to become a better fit for love's biological reality. This is one reason why I think it is crucial not to treat romantic love as purely a socially constructed phenomenon. Being able to see the complex back-and-forth between love's biology and its social role is important for understanding why these changes to the social role of love happen: why love breaks free from social constraints at the insistence of its biology.

Notice, though, that in order to understand the biology of love as a motivation for social change in this way, we need to rid our biological theory of love of the kind of ideology-driven assumptions that would cloud such understanding. The neurochemistry of love, we now know, looks much the same in queer and nonqueer lovers. This is part of the biological story of what love is, and it gives us a basis on which to argue for the social inclusion of queer love. But if we had always assumed love was restricted to hetero couples as a matter of biological necessity, we might never even have been motivated to research that question. Instead, we would have given ourselves a "biological" basis for rejecting the social inclusion of queer love without further investigation.

People have been excluded from the social role of romantic love for all kinds of reasons: queerness is one, along with belonging to different social classes, different religions, or different racialized groups. Dubious "biology" has frequently supplied excuses for such exclusion. And yet the real biology of love is precisely why none of these exclusive practices is ultimately sustainable. None of these social constraints on the role of romantic love have succeeded in preventing people from experiencing the rushes of adrenaline, dopamine, oxytocin, and so on. People (biologically speaking) keep falling in love even as they (socially speaking) are denied access to it.

You may now be wondering whether, if the biology of love insists like this, that means we should adopt an attitude of biological determinism. That is to say, should we conclude that the biology of love will eventually win out over any efforts we make at the social level to control or constrain it?

Lovers Gonna Love

We can summarize this attitude of biological determinism with the phrase "Lovers gonna love." This is shorthand for the idea that love just happens: it is a biological force of nature, under no one's control, and so we can't really do anything to change or contain it. If, for example, falling in love makes people obsessive, volatile, or dangerous to themselves or others, or if it makes women better nest makers and men better providers, then that's just how it is. Lovers gonna love.

Uncritical biological determinism is a dangerous business. Some people are biological determinists about gender roles too: they will say that men are biologically more competitive, aggressive, unfaithful, and so on than women, and nothing can change this because it's just the way men are. They can then use this idea to maintain and justify a status quo in which toxic behaviors get downplayed on the grounds that they are "only natural" and thus impossible to rein in. In fact, biological determinism about gender and biological determinism about love often go hand in hand: "Lovers gonna love" tends to line up neatly alongside "Boys will be boys."

At the extreme, versions of both can be deployed to justify or excuse violent crime. The idea of a crime of passion and the related legal defense of "provocation" have served disproportionately to secure lenience for men who violently killed or injured their adulterous wives and/or the men with whom their wives were being adulterous. The attitudes behind this have a long and sexist history. In England in the early eighteenth century, the lord chief justice called sex with another man's wife "the highest invasion of property" (because women were property) and said that since "jealousy is the rage of man," the violent killing of someone caught in the act of committing adultery with one's wife should not count as murder. In his own, more graphic words, "If the husband shall stab the adulterer, or knock out his brains, that is bare manslaughter."[4]

Attitudes have changed to some extent: for example, women are less often explicitly described as property now, at least not out loud, in public, by chief justices. In some contexts the law has changed too, though only quite recently. Since 2010, there is no longer a defense of "provocation" in UK law. The stated aim of this change was to "end the injustice of women being killed by their husband and then being blamed."[5] Canada restricted the provocation defense in 2015 to "those situations in which the victim's conduct constituted an indictable offence . . . punishable by five years or more in prison." This conduct must also be of the sort that would "deprive an ordinary person of the power of self-control," and the accused must have "acted on it on the sudden and before there was time for their passion to cool." Previously, Canadian law required only the second two conditions, which meant, in principle, that your husband might use legal actions you had every right to perform—such as saying something that made him think you were having an affair—as a partial legal defense for killing you.[6]

In the United States, the Model Penal Code does not explicitly use the word "provocation" but does permit leniency for killings committed "under the influence of extreme mental or emotional disturbance for which there is reasonable explanation or excuse."[7] This has enabled juries to reach verdicts of manslaughter (rather than murder) in cases where a man killed his wife or girlfriend and claimed "extreme mental or emotional disturbance" because she had left him, didn't love him, planned a divorce, danced with another man, and so forth.[8] The language of provocation is employed more directly in federal sentencing guidelines by the US Sentencing Commission, which allow that "if the victim's wrongful conduct contributed significantly to provoking the offense behavior, the court may reduce the sentence below the guideline range to reflect the nature and circumstances of the offense."[9]

Provocation also serves as an excuse for lethal violence against queer men. In England, men who turn violent when confronted with "sodomy" (especially of a son by another man) have used versions of the provocation defense for centuries. In contemporary cases, "gay panic" is a legal defense of provocation (or the equivalent) used to help excuse a straight-identifying man who kills a queer man after the latter has made an unwelcome advance. As law scholar Kyle Kirkup has pointed out,[10] killing someone out of anger specifically inspired by sexual orientation could be construed as a hate crime. Seen in this light, homophobia should be seen not as the basis for a legal defense but as the opposite: an aggravating factor.

Progress on these issues is slow. In 2014, California blocked uses of the "gay panic" defense and the corresponding "trans panic" defense (deployed in a similar way to excuse the killing of trans* people). The California Penal Code, which allows for a verdict of manslaughter in cases of killing "upon a sudden quarrel or heat of passion," was amended to note that "the provocation was not objectively reasonable if it resulted from the discovery of, knowledge about, or potential disclosure of the victim's actual or perceived gender, gender identity, gender expression, or sexual orientation, including under circumstances in which the victim made an unwanted nonforcible romantic or sexual advance towards the defendant."[11] The rest of the United States lacks such protections.

The pace of change is glacial because entrenched ways of thinking about "human nature"—especially when it comes to anything related to love, sex, or romance—are extremely resistant to change. Ingrained attitudes about what lovers are "naturally" like can be very difficult to remove fully from our nonconscious minds, even if we consciously disagree with them.[12] Meanwhile, romantic relationships continue to be significant sites of deadly violence—disproportionately for women. In 2013 in the United States, among female murder victims whose relationship to the killer was recorded, 36.6 percent were murdered by their male partners; 245 male murder victims were recorded as being the husband or boyfriend of their killer, while 992 female victims—over four times as many—were recorded as being the girlfriend or wife of their killer.[13]

What are we to do with this potentially dangerous "lovers gonna love" attitude that is so strongly associated with excusing violence? We need to tackle every claim about what is hardwired in us with critical thinking and moral judgment: critical thinking because some of these claims about hardwiring will just be false, and moral judgment because not everything that's "natural" is a good idea. We cure "natural" illnesses with artificial medical interventions. We make an effort to rise above our "natures" when there is good reason. When it comes to feeling angry enough to kill your unfaithful spouse, there is good reason. When it comes to excluding queer people from the social institution of romantic love, there is no legitimate reason at all. In both of these cases, I suspect "nature" is responsible for far less of what we observe than we've been encouraged to suppose. But we can only figure all this out through the exercise of critical thinking and moral judgment. We have to do that work. Biology isn't any kind of shortcut to an answer.

Only Biology Is Biology

Straightforward biological theorists of love place everything about love's nature on the biological side. For them, the deterministic thinking of "Lovers gonna love" is always within easy reach. Straightforward social constructionists place everything on the social side. They always have a ready argument against the idea that "lovers gonna love."

But the dual-nature theorist has neither of these simple options. The dual-nature theorist must figure out what belongs to the biology of love and what belongs to its social script. She can acknowledge that societies will never eradicate the biology of love in queer people just by excluding them from love at the social level, while simultaneously challenging the idea that male murderers should be treated leniently provided they were sufficiently enraged by their partners' behavior. I find it helpful to bear in mind the slogan "Only biology is biology." That's a tautology, of course, but it is also a way of focusing one's mind on this question of what really belongs on the biological side of the ledger and what doesn't. The brain chemistry of queer love does. Lenient sentencing for violent murderers does not.

When Helen Fisher claims that, as a matter of biological fact, romantic love evolved because our bipedal female ancestors were needy and had their hands full of babies, we should bear in mind that "only biology is biology." Associations between romantic love and female neediness may well turn out to fall on the social side of the ledger; the history of love is littered with attempts to attribute to "nature" what are really social prejudices. A trial judge whose ruling was appealed all the way to the US Supreme Court, resulting in the landmark case *Loving v. Virginia*, which in 1967 overturned antimiscegenation laws in the United States, had infamously attributed the prohibition of interracial marriage to the natural order of things (which, in turn, he attributed to divine will):[14]

> Almighty God created the races white, black, yellow, malay and red, and he placed them on separate continents. And, but for the interference with his arrangement, there would be no cause for such marriage. The fact that he separated the races shows that he did not intend for the races to mix.

In reality, the prohibition of interracial marriage is a chapter in the story of love's social role. Attempts to claim otherwise may look laughable now, but they are not ancient history: it was only in the mid-1990s that the approval rate for marriage between blacks and whites climbed to over 50 percent.[15]

Disappearing Love

There is a persistent idea that romantic love should unite two people of the same "kind" (with the exception of gender). This has been an important aspect of the social role of romantic love—and in some contexts it still is. The role has often built in restrictions to exclude love between people from different social classes, different religions, different racialized groups, and so on.

In 2001, clinical psychologist Maria Root published *Love's Revolution: Interracial Marriage*, based on analysis and interviews with around two hundred participants.[16] Root's discussion gives us clues as to how social attitudes to both interracial and same-sex relationships contribute to constructing the social role of romantic love. Although the two cases are different in many important ways (and intersect to create situations that are different again), Root notices an important similarity: among participants in her study, both kinds of relationships led to "legal consequences or the invocation of religion as a higher moral authority," and both "were often dismissed as merely sexual, as a way to undermine their legitimacy and potential for success and happiness." Here Root puts her finger on a common strategy for undermining the legitimacy and viability of any relationship that challenges the prevailing ideologies: the refusal to acknowledge love.

Love's social role is to take adult attraction and affection and output something resembling a stable nuclear family unit. Where there is resistance to the formation of family-like bonds between queer people or between people racialized into different groups, there is a corresponding resistance to the idea of romantic love between such people. This can take the form of mere disapproval, but even more powerfully, it can take the form of denials that such love is so much as possible. This then leads to the conclusion that any queer or interracial relationship must really be a matter of sexual attraction alone. Because of negative attitudes toward sex in general, this incurs disapproval and disrespect. The desired— and likely—consequence is that, under such pressure and without the normal social supports, the relationship will be unable to fulfill the social function of creating a stable family unit. In terms of Beall and Sternberg's social constructionism (explored back in chapter 2), we can identify this as one of society's regulative mechanisms for stamping out disfavored manifestations of love.

In order to fully understand these refusals to acknowledge love, we need to appreciate their significance in terms of what love is (i.e., what love does) at the social level. Sometimes denials of love are obvious and deliberate, explicitly overriding what the lovers themselves say. Family members may simply tell a queer or interracial couple that they aren't in love—that it's just lust, confusion, or the work of Satan. There are also subtler, more insidious ways of making love disappear, just by failing to acknowledge its very possibility. But they all serve the same end: averting disruptions to the current social structure. Changing love means changing our social world and, as such, will always be unwelcome in many quarters.

By looking at the recent history of interracial love and queer love, we can identify some major changes to romantic love's social role (and corresponding disruptions to prevailing social arrangements). There have been and will be others. But these are enough to draw our attention to an important conceptual question: If the role of romantic love defines what romantic love is at the social level, then shouldn't any change to the role mean that romantic love gets destroyed and replaced with something else? How can romantic love be one thing over time if it is under constant construction and reconstruction?

Well, many things—indeed, most things—change over time while remaining one and the same thing. You, for example, can change your hair color or your opinions without becoming a different person. Change is normal and doesn't always amount to replacing one thing with another. It's no different for socially constructed things. Take the game of soccer, for example. It is a social construct: we make it what it is by deciding on its rules and traditions. Yet the game of soccer can clearly change over time, acquiring different rules. We still think of it as one and the same game that persists throughout these changes.

So why exactly do we say soccer is a single game that has changed over time as opposed to one that is destroyed and replaced with a different game every time there is a rule change? It's because of two factors. First, the changes are small and happen gradually, not in huge leaps. Second, these small, gradual changes take place against a background of constancy: at any given time, the majority of the rules of soccer aren't changing, and this allows for some adjustments at the edges.

The same goes for the social role of romantic love. We couldn't replace every aspect of love's social role at once and still count it as the same phenomenon we had before. But we can make small, gradual changes against a background of constancy. This is then love evolving, not being destroyed and replaced.

We should predict that romantic love will continue to change, as it always has. One person, book, or movie won't change the social role of love overnight; the changes will be gradual. But they will happen. And this is one reason why understanding the dual nature of love is so important. Armed only with an understanding of love's biology, we are liable to conceive of love as a natural, objective, and unchanging thing over which we have relatively little influence. This strips us of the conceptual resources to predict and responsibly plan for the ways love is going to change at the social level. So we end up stumbling through those changes without awareness.

On the flip side, armed only with an understanding of love as a social construct, we would lack valuable insights into the kinds of changes that might actually work and represent a better fit, given the kinds of creatures we are. For instance, we might want to effect social change so that we came to collectively represent romantic love as the kind of thing one can "just snap out of" when a relationship ends instead of experiencing months of heartbreak. But the biological reality is that many people undergo significant chemical changes in their brains when bonding romantically with others, and these have profound and lasting effects. Making these biological love bonds cancellable at will just by altering our social norms isn't an option. Our biology puts some limits on what social change can achieve and gives us clues as to when and how such change can succeed.

In the future, we may find ways of interfering with the biology of love directly using drugs or more radical interventions. (I'll have more to say about that later.) But we won't find a way to circumvent the vitally important work of understanding love's dual nature. Only by appreciating this duality can we hope to figure out, when love is going wrong, whether the problems stem from society, biology, or a failure of fit between the two.

This work must be done because, as things stand, romantic love is failing us in multiple ways. Let's take a look at some of them.

What Needs to Change

6

I strain my heart, I stretch my hands,
And catch at hope.

—Christina Rossetti, *De Profundis*

Abjectly Obedient Women, and Other Sweet Love Stories

They say that love and marriage go together like a horse and carriage. The horse-drawn carriage resulted from artificially harnessing a biological organism to an invented technology. The pairing was a success because it suited certain purposes that people had in a particular social context at a particular period in history. Times have changed though: nowadays horses and carriages are rarely seen together. Carriages have evolved into cars. As for the biological half of the pairing, it hasn't changed much: horses are still pretty much just horses, relieved of their carriage-pulling duties.

At a particular period in history, for certain purposes, some societies harnessed romantic love to "traditional" marriage. I put scare quotes around "traditional" here because it only recently became "traditional" in European culture to marry for love. Marriage was more traditionally a property transaction, in which a man gave a woman to another man. This doesn't mean love in marriage was unknown; of course, love can arise even in relationships that began as property transactions. But we should be wary of reading too much romance into apparently adorable stories of spousal love from a bygone age.

In *The Marriage Book*, Lisa Grunwald and Stephen Adler present one such story, which they describe as one of "the most extraordinary gifts of inspiration."[1] It is a story told by a Roman man in his eulogy for his wife. He describes their excellent marriage, his affection for his wife, and his grief at her death. The centerpiece of the story is that because the couple was childless, this most dutiful of wives offered to divorce her husband and even to bring him another woman to have children with. (She is assumed to be the infertile member of the couple.) She would then help raise these children, taking on the "duties and the loyalty of a sister and mother-in-law."

What a striking act of loving self-sacrifice, we're invited to think. But on closer evaluation, we might notice how much the eulogy emphasizes the wife's "loyalty" and "obedience." These are the first entries in a long list of her "domestic virtues." And we might notice that the husband has a temper, which he says "flared up such that I almost lost control of myself" when she offered to find him another woman. In fact, his loss of control in the face of extreme emotion is a recurring theme in the eulogy:

he also mentions that owing to his wife's death, he is subject to grief that "wrests away [his] power of self-control."

We only have one perspective on this relationship. The husband was clearly pleased with it. We are left to wonder what the wife might have said, if she could speak to us without worrying what would happen if her husband heard her and lost control of his emotions again. I hesitate to call a relationship explicitly grounded in the "obedience" and abject self-sacrifice of one of its members an inspirational example of ancient romantic love.

It is, in fact, a salutary reminder of how ancient gender stereotypes somehow look more acceptable when we see them through the rose-tinted lens of a sweet love story. If we unthinkingly recycle and romanticize the idea that abject obedience is the highest virtue of a woman in love, we facilitate women's abuse and oppression within romantic relationships. The gender stereotype that infuses this Roman man's conception of a good wife is still with us thousands of years later. It is an aspect of the social role of romantic love that needs to change.

If You Liked It, Then You Should Have Put a Ring on It— and Earned More Than Her

In our own era, romantic love is so strongly associated with marriage that in 2015 the US Supreme Court's ruling on marriage equality was announced in phrases like "Love just won" (President Barack Obama's Facebook status update on the day) and #lovewins (which quickly became a top-trending hashtag on Twitter). An alien visiting Earth could reasonably have concluded that love and marriage are basically the same thing around here. Indeed, the language of the Supreme Court ruling confirms this impression:

> No union is more profound than marriage, for it embodies the highest ideals of love, fidelity, devotion, sacrifice, and family . . . [M]arriage embodies a love that may endure even past death. . . . [The] hope [of the petitioners in this case] is not to be condemned to live in loneliness, excluded from one of civilization's oldest institutions. They ask for equal dignity in the eyes of the law. The Constitution grants them that right.

This passage can sound sweet at first glance. But read again, and you see how the alternative to marriage (i.e., the alternative to love) is a life of loneliness. That message is dark, and it is not subtle. When we celebrate this statement as a beautiful piece of contemporary wisdom, we demonstrate once again that we are willing to swallow quite disturbing ideas, provided they are packaged for us in sweet love stories.

It's true that in some parts of Europe and North America, living "in sin" with a partner to whom one is not married is nowhere near as stigmatized as it was in Bertrand Russell's day. But the idea that love is supposed to lead to marriage is still a central feature of contemporary social life, as will be familiar to anyone who has seen a few rom coms, felt the pressure of families asking, "When are you two going to get married," or understood what Beyoncé meant when she said, "If you liked it, then you should have put a ring on it."

The assumption that love and marriage are basically the same thing—or would be if you were doing life right—is damaging to the people who are in love and still unable to marry, who are in love and have no wish to marry, and who are married but receive only abuse from their spouses. This normative conflation of love with marriage is another aspect of the romantic love role that needs to change.

This is not a wholly separate problem from the gender stereotyping; in fact, the two are intimately connected. For the last couple of hundred years, romantic love has been supposed to lead not just to marriage but to a particular gendered marital arrangement: the husband works outside the home and participates in public life, while the wife provides free, unlimited child care and domestic labor. These are not dead stereotypes. In hetero marriages, women are still held responsible for the majority of child care and housework by default, even if they also work outside the home. Women do significantly more housework across the board than men do.[2] Men face a corresponding default expectation that they will "provide" financially.

In a 2015 paper in the *Quarterly Journal of Economics*, Marianne Bertrand, Emir Kamenica, and Jessica Pan illustrate the tenacity of the idea that a wife should not earn more than her husband.[3] They analyze income data from the United States ranging from 1970 to 2011. In the data for 1970, the wife's earnings very commonly made up less than 10 percent of household income. From 1980 onward, the share of household income earned by the wife expanded to be pretty much anything, provided it was below 50 percent. Even in the most recent data (covering the 2008–2011 period), it is quite unusual for the wife to earn more than half the household income. If the wife does earn more than half, she most likely brings in only slightly more.[4]

Hetero married couples seem strongly resistant to arrangements in which the wife earns significantly more than the husband. The gender pay gap reinforces this status quo. (In the United States, women on average earn seventy-eight cents for every dollar earned by a man.[5])

Worse still, Bertrand and her coauthors' analysis of the data indicates that the few wives who do earn more than their husbands also tend to do more of the housework and child care than their husbands: they take on a "second shift" when they get home.[6] The authors hypothesize that this represents an attempt to "compensate" for the threat they pose to gender roles. Perhaps unsurprisingly in light of this, they also find that these arrangements lead to lower marital satisfaction and a greater likelihood of divorce.

Gendered assumptions about how a romantic relationship is supposed to look can have a significant impact on our lives even if we don't notice it. One fascinating study by psychologists Laurie Rudman and Jessica Heppen found that women who thought of their romantic partners in terms of "chivalry and heroism" (i.e., as knights in shining armor) were on average less interested in pursuing high-status occupations for themselves and less ambitious when it came to earnings, education, and leadership goals.[7] (Men's romantic associations did not exhibit any such correlation.) But here's the thing: only the women's implicit—unstated and possibly unconscious—associations predicted lowered ambition, not their explicit romantic fantasies. Rudman and Heppen conclude that their research confirms the existence of a "glass slipper" effect: socialization into romantic gender norms leaves women's ambitions tottering and limping along but operates below the level of conscious awareness. It is hard to see the glass slippers on our own feet.[8]

Saving Love from Itself with Simone de Beauvoir

Feminist philosophers have been discussing romantic love's connections to gender for a long time. In "The Woman in Love," a chapter in her 1949 book *The Second Sex*, Simone de Beauvoir makes the case that patriarchal romantic love encourages women to seek self-annihilation through absorption into the identity of a male partner.[9] For de Beauvoir, an existentialist, this is anathema to an "authentic" life.

Importantly, though, de Beauvoir believed the damaging gender roles associated with romantic love to be changeable. In her view, they are not "hardwired" into us as part of our biology because gender roles in general are not "hardwired." De Beauvoir was an intellectual pioneer in developing the idea that gender roles are socially constructed. I want to build on that idea by saying that, in the process of constructing gender roles, we are simultaneously constructing some of romantic love's contours. As a result, love itself is gendered at the social level: strong patterns emerge in the composite image of love, prescribing different experiences of love for women and for men. Of course in some instances individuals engage in gender role reversal. But the fact that there is reversal shows that the gender roles are there and ready to be reversed.

De Beauvoir thought that romantic gender roles could be transformed into something more positive. Shulamith Firestone, a later feminist author, was not so optimistic. In her 1970 book *The Dialectic of Sex*, Firestone called romantic love "love corrupted by its power context" and "a diseased form of love" intended to reinforce the power imbalance between men and women.[10] As she saw it, advances in civilization were destroying the biological basis for that power imbalance, so it had become necessary to shore it up with social institutions. Firestone thought romantic love was one such institution, along with the patriarchal nuclear family. For this reason, she called romanticism "a cultural tool of male power to keep women from knowing their condition." She thought it was unsalvageable.

Even today harmful gender stereotypes are associated with romantic love. Should we conclude, with Firestone, that romantic love is unsalvageable? Or should we follow de Beauvoir in thinking it can become something better?

I'm with de Beauvoir here. Social constructs are real, but they are also dynamic. In fact, looking back at Firestone's work gives us some traction on this point. Firestone defined romantic love as "love between the sexes." This was not unusual in the 1970s and earlier. But the social construction of romantic love has already moved on to the point where this definition looks overly narrow; same-sex love is now much more likely to be included.

Like the normative connection between love and marriage, romantic love's association with heteronormativity has been connected to its reinforcement of gender roles. If it's not necessary for love to involve one woman and one man, how can it be necessary for it to involve one stereotypically womanly woman and one stereotypically manly man? In fact, seen in the right light, heteronormativity is just a form of romantic gender stereotyping:

the "script" for romantic love used to have two clearly defined roles for two clearly defined genders. Start to question that, and you simultaneously challenge both heteronormativity and sexist assumptions about romance. It's a two-for-one deal.

Still, it takes time and effort—not to mention luck and good timing—to change anything about the social role of romantic love. Persuading people to part with their cherished ideas about it is hard, but any progress is exciting, and we have witnessed some relatively rapid change of late. Large-scale moves toward the inclusion of same-sex love have happened around me in my lifetime, and comparable moves toward the inclusion of interracial love were happening in the lives of the generation before me.

Philosophical reflection on love's nature is timely precisely because romantic love is in a period of such overhaul. Right now we are poised to learn the lesson that love can change dramatically at the social level. Armed with that information, we can begin to identify what still needs to change, and we can get to work. Romantic gender stereotyping, the heteronormativity that still lingers, and the assumption that love should lead to marriage are high on the list—and they are all interconnected.

One crucial first step toward positive change is appreciating that romantic love is not straightforwardly an individual or private matter. You cannot close the doors of a home around a romantic relationship and imagine that this prevents society from intruding. On the contrary, we bring it right in with us. We literally bring into our homes the rom coms, romance novels, poetry, and myriad other representations that contribute to our composite image of what love is. We figuratively bring in all the expectations for a "normal relationship" that we have been absorbing ever since we joined in playground renditions of the K-I-S-S-I-N-G rhyme.

Taking charge, consciously, of the possibilities for change requires that we first appreciate the sense in which it "takes a village" to fall in love.

All Else Being Equal

I have been able to watch the composite image of romantic love change over my lifetime. Representations of queer love have become much more common and much closer to "normal," and as a result heteronormativity is no longer such a strong emergent contour in the composite image. Even so, internalized heteronormativity is hard to shift, which I can attest to on a personal level. I was over thirty before I noticed a strange disparity: I was dating women and men and had an online dating profile that mentioned that I was attracted to women, but it had never occurred to me to update my profile—or my self-conception—to anything other than "straight." Once I noticed the disparity, I found it funny—but the point is, I did not notice it for a long time. I had been so strongly conditioned to assume I was straight that I kept doing so, even in the face of fairly compelling evidence to the contrary.

Although we live in interesting times when it comes to love's social role, change happens against a backdrop of continuity. This continuity is not necessarily a bad thing, and it's part of what makes romantic love one thing over time (something that persists through change rather than being destroyed and replaced). But it means that efforts to include same-sex love have often involved emphasizing that doing so helps promote other romantic norms, especially the norm of monogamy.

Monogamy is currently a central feature in the social role of romantic love. That role is about harnessing adult affection and attraction into stable nuclear family units, which have a two-person nucleus. One effective strategy in arguing for the inclusion of queer love has been to show that romantic love can perform its social function better if it gets to work on the affection and attraction between two queer folks as well as that between two straight ones. It can output more monogamous nuclear family units that way, leaving fewer potentially disruptive instances of attraction and affection that fall outside its remit. Emphasizing the existence and moral rights of same-sex monogamous couples, who are a relatively good fit for the current romantic love role, opened up the possibility of making this small change while maintaining and even enhancing the other elements of love's social function.

For this reason, progress toward the inclusion of same-sex love has often been premised on emphatic assurances of the continued exclusion of polyamory. This is another thing that needs to change. Stigma against nonmonogamous love is pervasive and unreasonable; psychologist Terri Conley and coauthors recently conducted a study that found "monogamous relationships were rated more positively than CNM [consensual nonmonogamous] relationships on every dimension," including with respect to factors wholly irrelevant to monogamy. For example, they found that monogamous individuals are perceived as being more likely to floss daily and reliably walk their dogs than individuals in consensual nonmonogamous relationships. "Across all studies," they report, "the results consistently demonstrated stigma surrounding CNM and a halo effect surrounding monogamy."[11]

However, this kind of halo effect is not always obvious to the people who enjoy its benefits. In a conversation about why she felt it was important to do this research, Conley describes how people would tell her monogamy was really the stigmatized option: "They said, *Well, in Hollywood non-monogamy is all people do, so it's monogamy that's stigmatized.* . . . I always think that's such a crazy situation, when the dominant group actually thinks it's being persecuted."[12] Whatever is true in Hollywood, most of us do not live there. For us, the stigma and social rejection that surround nonmonogamy carry costs that are hard to count. My boyfriend's father refuses to talk to him about anything except the weather until he breaks up with me.[13] We've been together for years, and I've never met any of his family.

But rejection is not the only problem. If I had children, I'd be concerned that my poly relationships could be used as grounds for taking them away from me. I often wonder whether it would be legal for someone to fire me, or refuse to let me stay at a hotel, or incite violence against me on the grounds that I have two romantic partners. I'm happy to say those things haven't happened to me, but when I've discussed my relationships in popular media, I've received enough anonymous feedback wishing bad things on me to make me conscious of safety issues. Moreover, in many parts of the world adultery is illegal; in some it is punishable by death. In the United States, at least, the anti-adultery laws are rarely enforced.[14] But it's not exactly comfortable to know that I could be a criminal in the United States when I only wanted to be a tourist.

All the stigma surrounding nonmonogamous relationships has given queer activism a strong pragmatic reason to distance itself from nonmonogamy and promote a narrative of queer love that very closely resembles "traditional" monogamous romance. Queer poly people are particularly at risk in this dynamic, becoming liable to be told that they are "ruining gay marriage for everybody"[15] and excluded from queer communities on top of already facing multiple forms of stigmatization.

The rush to keep romantic love monogamous is not restricted to queer activism, of course. It has been joined from all sides. Social conservatives are motivated to join by the sentiment behind Jean-Luc Picard's famous ultimatum: "The line must be drawn here. This far, no further!"[16] US conservative Eli Lehrer wrote a *HuffPost* blog post in 2013 that appeared under the not overly subtle headline "Gay Marriage Good, Polyamory Bad."[17] In it, Lehrer explains that "gay marriage is, at the very worst, neutral for society while polyamory is pretty clearly harmful to society." The article is hard to read in a number of ways; Lehrer is the kind of writer who will drop in a phrase like "handful of backward Muslims" without missing a beat. More relevant for current purposes, though, is what Lehrer thinks polyamory is. In one revealing passage he says, "Polyamorous societies will, by definition, never have enough mates to go around"; he adds, "Always and everywhere, this has resulted in significant numbers of disaffected heterosexual males who have no hope of finding a mate."

By definition? Lehrer is thinking of patriarchal polygamy, in which men can have multiple wives but the reverse arrangement is not permitted. The people he refers to as "mates" are, to be more accurate, women. It is simply not on Lehrer's radar that women could ever have multiple partners. This mistake alone means that Lehrer's argument makes no contact with its purported target: he is not discussing polyamory; he is discussing patriarchal polygamy.

When Lehrer considers whether there are enough "mates" to go around, he concludes that leaving distribution to the free market would inevitably lead to some men not receiving their share. His concern is that those men will become "disaffected" and then (presumably) bash things or upset the social order. The argument is not original to Lehrer; it is a perennial trope. I'm interested not in the failed argument per se but in the attitudes to gender that are revealed when people discuss monogamy in these terms.

There are a number of issues to untangle. First, Lehrer seems to think that men who are romantically frustrated are a terrible and dangerous force of nature that no one can or should control. Perhaps I'm overly optimistic, but I don't think this is justified. I give men more credit than that: I think they are capable of self-control, and I don't assume violence is the inevitable consequence when they don't get the women they want or feel they deserve.

In addition to the misandry, there's a strange conception of women—or "mates"—as a kind of property or commodity that ought to be distributed among hetero men in an equitable manner. Only once one is thinking of women that way could it make sense to think of there not being enough to "go around." Only then could one countenance the legal enforcement of a redistributive policy that would interfere with individual liberty.

Another well-known redistributive policy, structurally parallel to Lehrer's, maintains that we shouldn't permit significant financial inequality. After all, financially inegalitarian societies will, by definition, never have enough money to go around. Always and everywhere, this has resulted in significant numbers of disaffected people who have no hope of acquiring wealth. Should we conclude that, because of the damage the disaffected poor may do to the fabric of society, the state should intervene to limit how much wealth any one individual may acquire? This would radically interfere with individual liberty, of course, but Lehrer seems to think that serious state intervention is appropriate to ensure a proper distribution of resources in such situations.

This analogy helps highlight the fundamental mistake behind the argument. Wealth may or may not be a commodity suitable for state redistribution, but women definitely are not. In untangling this kind of philosophical mess, that is the most important thread to pull on. The rest of it unravels as soon as we do that.

The Status of Sluts

While we're on the subject of money, wealth and social class are themselves important for understanding romantic love's social function. For a number of reasons, people are more likely to choose romantic partners of a similar socioeconomic status (especially education level) to their own.[18] Major changes to this norm would present destabilizing risks to a society, as widespread love-based marriage across status divisions would encourage greater social mobility as well as serve to highlight the arbitrariness and injustice of status distinctions in the first place.

Nevertheless, it has long been accepted that romantic love can in exceptional cases cross barriers of class, wealth, and status. This idea might be as old as romantic love itself: Cinderella-like folktales have been around for centuries at least. (Notice, though, that the genders in the Cinderella story are a big part of its "romantic" appeal: high-status women who marry low-status men are not viewed in quite the same light.) The social institution of "morganatic" marriage—in which a lower-status spouse and any offspring of the marriage are prohibited from inheriting property and/or titles from a higher-status spouse—attempts to alleviate some of the destabilizing impacts of love between partners of very different status. The rate at which people marry outside their own social class varies with time and circumstance.[19] But the basic idea that love can conquer all has never really gone away. In some ways, it has served as a model for "love-conquers-all" narratives in other arenas (such as interracial and same-sex love).

Class status also has subtler influences on how romantic love works. For example, it affects the ways in which one is liable to be penalized for violating romantic norms. Sociologists have recently studied the relationship between slut shaming and social class among college women, finding that high-status women would call low-status women "slutty" in order to "assert class advantage" and "defin[e] themselves as classy rather than trashy."[20] Violations of the norm of romantic monogamy are commonly policed via the mechanism of slut shaming. The findings of this study thus suggest that violating the norm of monogamy is likely to carry a lesser penalty for those protected by higher social class.[21]

It also carries a higher penalty for women than for men. I call this the "slut-versus-stud phenomenon." It's not hard to come up with a long and colorful list of words that specifically denigrate promiscuous women. But what words denigrate promiscuous men? A "rake" or "cad" sounds like the dashing antihero in a P. G. Wodehouse story. A "playboy" or "player" sounds like somebody who has a lot of fun. A "pimp" is a man who controls or manages sex workers, not someone who is himself promiscuous. I've never heard anyone use the word "gigolo" in real life. "Man-whore" is explicitly a masculinized version of a feminine word. "Womanizer" might be the best candidate, but while derogatory it lacks the vitriolic punch of "slut" (partly because it points to an activity rather than an identity). And I don't know of any words generally used to praise promiscuous women in a manner comparable to the way "stud" is used for men.

The use of slut shaming to penalize women, especially lower-status women, for (perceived) failures of monogamy is a blunt weapon. The concept of "sluttiness" targets only sex, not love or relationships. In fact, however, this makes it all the more effective, because it serves to reinforce the idea that nonmonogamous relationships don't count as love: they are really just sex. This is a common strategy for making disfavored forms of love disappear, thus reinforcing the exclusive contours of love's social role.

With any movement that aims to make romantic love more inclusive at the social level, there is a threat to social stability. In addition to the general instability associated with change of any kind, love has a special place in defining who we think we are and how we think we should live. Expanding the social role of romantic love to include interracial relationships is highly destabilizing to a social order that is rigidly segregated on racial lines. The inclusion of same-sex love—and, more generally, challenging established romantic gender roles—is similarly destabilizing to a social order that expects wives to provide domestic labor for husbands who work outside the home.

Nonmonogamous love is interestingly different, however: it poses distinctive destabilizing risks that strike directly at the heart of romantic love's social function, whatever kind of social order it is embedded within. If the social role of romantic love allowed for polyamorous love, it could obviously become much less effective at performing its core function of channeling affection and attraction into stable nuclear family–like units. Many kinds of queer and interracial love can be brought to fit the mold of the nuclear family. Others can't, but these have been successfully downplayed in the push for greater acceptance. With poly love, it's just too obvious that many or most forms cannot be squeezed into the confines of the nuclear mold. While some poly people form nuclear families, polyamory encompasses infinite possible configurations, and many of them blatantly fail to conform to anything like the nuclear model.

First Comes Love, Then Comes Marriage, Then Comes Baby in a Baby Carriage

Because change happens against a backdrop of continuity, the inclusion of same-sex love in the social role of romantic love has been promoted by reaffirming the norm of monogamy. A parallel—but even less visible—phenomenon has been the reaffirmation of amatonormativity (introduced earlier as the idea that romantic love is ideal and a default for everyone) as part of the backdrop to this change.

Just like normative monogamy, amatonormativity can be deployed to help show how romantic love can better accomplish its social role if we make a relatively small change to include same-sex cases. Here, the thought is that we can more successfully prescribe romantic love as the ideal state for everyone if we allow for same-sex love. That way, those for whom hetero love is not an option can still be expected to conform to amatonormative pressure. Recall how the US Supreme Court ruling on same-sex marriage snuck in the message that the alternative to marriage is to be "condemned to live in loneliness."

Once again, predictably, amatonormativity impacts differently according to gender. While men may aspire to the status of "confirmed bachelor," women are given the prospect of becoming a "crazy old cat lady." Even the simple word "spinster" suggests a dull, sexless woman who is probably deeply weird in some way: if you're lucky, Miss Marple; if you're unlucky, Miss Havisham.[22]

Amatonormativity is so common that it usually passes unremarked; even extreme versions of it won't so much as raise an eyebrow. And I don't just mean in café conversations, rom coms, or pop songs (though let's not overlook the powerful messages conveyed in lyrics like "You're Nobody 'til Somebody Loves You"). Casual amatonormativity is routine even in scholarly research.

For example, in a recent article discussing the theoretical comparison of romantic love to addiction, Michel Reynaud and coauthors describe "love passion" as "a universal and necessary state for human beings."[23] Note the wording: passionate love is not just common; it is "universal." And it's not just nice but also "necessary." Now imagine—or perhaps this is already true of you and you don't have to imagine—that you have not been in love and have no plans to be; you are happy in your relationships with your family and friends and community, and you don't think romantic love is something you want in your own life. These scientists, in a single sentence, have both theorized you out of existence and classified your life as inadequate.

Amatonormativity is so pervasive as to be more or less invisible except to the people it most directly affects. For everyone else, it's become like wallpaper: however strange and ugly the pattern is, it's there every minute of every day. If you have no reason to notice it, you won't. If we truly want to permit and respect a diversity of life choices, we need to work at removing amatonormativity from our composite image of romantic love.

But just as with monogamy, any challenge to amatonormativity poses a distinctive destabilizing risk that goes to the heart of romantic love's social function. If romantic love works to channel adult affection and attraction into stable nuclear family units, it is necessary to guard against people ending up with either multiple romantic partners or none at all. The former task falls to the norm of monogamy, the latter to amatonormativity. They are like twin gutters whose job is to keep us all rolling down the same alley toward the same pins.

They are also some of the hardest aspects of love's social role to see clearly, precisely because they are some of the most fundamental. Social stability—including the maintenance of privilege by the privileged—is best served by mass unawareness of the deep core of the social machinery that structures our lives and our loves.

It is even more effective if we can attribute these deep-core norms to "nature" or "biology" so that we'll accept them as inevitable.

To round off this discussion, let me mention one more aspect of love's current social role that needs to change. At the moment, there are strong normative connections between love and reproduction: specifically, the production of biological offspring within a (hetero) marriage. My experience of becoming a recently married woman in my early thirties came with a widespread expectation that I would soon be having biological kids with my husband.

This default expectation that biological kids are on the horizon as soon as love becomes serious—and especially once a couple is married—can cause harm, both to adults and to children. It can lead people to have kids simply because it's expected rather than because it's desired, and it imposes a sense of inadequacy or failure on those who do not want or cannot have biological children.

Like all the other issues we've looked at in this chapter, the reproductive norm is gendered too. As Bertrand Russell pointed out back in 1929, though, it's far from obvious that it is gendered the right way around. Russell noticed that people seemed to think women wanted children more than men did, but he said, "My own impression, for what it's worth, is exactly the contrary. . . . A woman, after all, has to face labour and pain and possible loss of beauty in order to bring a child into the world, whereas a man has no such grounds for anxiety."[24] It turns out that statistics confirm his suspicion. Economist Marina Adshade pointed out in a 2015 article in the *Globe and Mail* that the Statistics Canada General Social Survey has for decades now included data on how Canadians answer the question, "How many children do you plan to have, including the ones that have already been born or you are expecting at this time?"[25] The question was first asked in 1990; back then, more men than women said they wanted children, regardless of age or marital status.

However, by 2011 the percentage of men who didn't want children had almost doubled. Adshade has a hypothesis about this, based on something that never seems to have occurred to Russell as a possibility: men taking responsibility for child care. Adshade's diagnosis of the data is simply that "men have always wanted babies as long as women were willing to make all the sacrifices. Now that those sacrifices are more evenly shared between parents, no one should be surprised to learn that fewer men now want to have children."

A more general moral is worth drawing out here. What is normative—in the sense of being socially prescribed—does not have to be statistically normal. Women normatively want children more than men do, but it doesn't follow that this pattern is statistically normal. Likewise, the perfect cereal-box nuclear family— the normatively prescribed life choice—is actually a rare thing. Perhaps this shouldn't be surprising: if it were truly "natural" and desirable for all or even most of us, we would hardly need all these social norms and penalties to channel everyone toward it.[26]

Changing the Composite Image

In my time and place, the social role of romantic love—a composite image that emerges from the overlaying of all our cultural representations, norms, and narratives—builds in some features that are causing harm and need to change. I've reviewed just a few in this chapter: the normative assumption that love should lead to marriage and biological reproduction; the norm of romantic monogamy; amatonormativity; and, permeating all of these while also contributing further harms of their own, the stereotypical gender roles for romantic love.

These social norms work together to make romantic love a powerful force for the creation of "traditional" nuclear family units, causing tangible damage to anyone caught in the cross-hairs. The nuclear family model works well for a lot of people. When it succeeds for you and the people you know, it can be nice to imagine that success writ large as a template for everyone's life. In fact, this imaginative projection can be so gratifying that it becomes unsettling and even scary to imagine accepting any-thing else as "normal." But when we get down to it, the nuclear family simply does not have the right to disparage or erase every other model of what a good life can look like.

One theme underlies all the changes I'm advocating for here. None of them involves restricting the role of romantic love or excluding anybody from it who is currently included. If you are hetero and monogamous and want a completely "traditional" marriage, then I say go for it. The social role of romantic love should be fully open to you so that you can freely choose that option. In fact, you can only ever choose that option freely if the norms that force your hand are dissolved. If "traditional" is the only flavor of relationship readily available to you, ending up with it isn't exactly a choice. It is more like Henry Ford's fabled offer of a Model T in "any color so long as it's black."

In the next chapter I turn to the future of love (by way of some of its history). We are constantly adding more and more layers to our composite image of what love is. Old layers are fading out. We could ultimately dissolve each of the damaging features of love's social role if we wanted to.

But even granting that these changes to the social role of love are individually possible, could we really make all of them? Would there be anything left of romantic love if we did that? And while all this was going on at the social level, what could— or should—we do about love at the level of biology?

7

It's Love, Jim, but Not as We Know It: The Future (via the Past)

Twenty love-sick maidens we,
Love-sick all against our will.
Twenty years hence we shall be
Twenty love-sick maidens still.

—W. S. Gilbert, *Patience*

Too Much Serenity Is Not Good for You

I know it's cheesy, but I will confess that I like the Serenity Prayer. We all need serenity to accept what we cannot change and courage to change what we can. We also need wisdom to know the difference.

"While we cannot alter the nature of love," write psychiatrists Thomas Lewis, Fari Amini, and Richard Lannon, "we can choose to defy its dictates or thrive within its walls. Those with the wisdom to do so will heed their hearts." They develop this philosophical thesis in their book *A General Theory of Love*.[1] They are talking not about romantic love specifically but about loving attachment in general. In their view, loving attachment is rooted in the "limbic system," a grouping of brain structures associated with emotion and motivation.[2] But Lewis and his coauthors emphasize the role of art, as well as science, in a full understanding of love. "Both are metaphors," they say, "through which we strive to know the world and ourselves."

A General Theory is a great read in many ways, and I am sympathetic to this methodological effort to harness both arts and sciences. But it is unsatisfying to me for several reasons. For one thing, the theory does not account for romantic love's dual nature; it neglects the socially constructed aspect. (While the authors consider art as a source of clues, the only serious account of love's nature on offer is one about brain systems.) For another, the idea that love is ultimately only approachable through metaphor— especially in combination with the idea that we cannot successfully defy its nature and must accept it if we want to "thrive within its walls"—is an analogue of the romantic mystique, something we need to move beyond. The theory I'm offering in this book is not a metaphor (although I sometimes use metaphors in an attempt to make the theory more comprehensible). I am trying to discover and tell the literal truth about romantic love to the best of my ability.

Crucially, I don't subscribe to the idea that we cannot alter the nature of love. Romantic love, at least, we can change. We are constantly refining and redefining its social nature. The process is slow and not always perceptible to the casual observer, but incremental change is always happening. It becomes easier to see when we reflect on how different, socially, romantic love is now compared to a hundred years ago.

It's vital that we become aware of this, because we share a collective responsibility for how the process goes on. We have a responsibility to make romantic love a force for good: to make sure our changes to the "script" direct love toward becoming a better version of itself. Resorting to deterministic thinking—there's nothing we can do, no change we can make—is a way of abdicating our responsibility. It is treating damaging romantic stereotypes as a force of nature that we can neither control nor change, throwing up our hands and saying, "Lovers gonna love." It is an excess of serenity.

Even a biological theorist of love shouldn't buy this deterministic attitude, because it's now becoming clear that it is possible to alter the nature of love at the biological as well as the social level. In fact, this idea has a venerable history.

Kinds of Magic

Serious interventions into the biology of love are only recently starting to sound realistic. But the idea of inducing or curing love with potions, lotions, balms, ointments, or basically anything we can get our hands on is an ancient one. It's been pervasive in art, literature, and medicine for thousands of years. While it's complicated to assume that anything like the current social role of romantic love existed in the ancient world, the biology of love certainly did. And people wanted to control it, even if that meant resorting to magic.[3]

Perhaps this possibility has such a grip on our collective imagination because the ability to control someone's love is a powerful thing. When it comes to plot construction, at any rate, love magic is a gift that keeps on giving. Think of that episode of *Buffy the Vampire Slayer* in which Buffy's goofy male friend Xander gets the entire female population of Sunnydale High chasing him around; or Donizetti's *L'elisir d'amour*, in which naive villager Nemorino purchases a highly priced love potion from a "doctor" of dubious credentials (this particular love potion—an inexpensive Bordeaux—turns out to be quite effective); or *Harry Potter and the Half-Blood Prince*, which features both a "love" potion and its antidote.

Love potions stay fresh as plot devices because they tap into a long-standing fascination with altering the biology of love. That idea isn't confined to fiction, though. When treated as a genuine possibility, it becomes even more fascinating: it reveals a lot about how we understand love, life, and the human condition. If biological interventions into love are indeed our future, we will be better prepared to face it if we know something of the relevant past.

For centuries, it was believed that body and mind alike were regulated by four "humors," or bodily fluids: blood, phlegm, black bile, and yellow bile. The ancient Greek physician Hippocrates—who gave his name to the Hippocratic oath—formalized this idea, though it probably originated even earlier. Although modern science has left the four humors theory behind, it still resonates in our vocabulary: when we describe someone as "melancholy," for example, we are attributing to that individual the kind of temperament once thought to result from an excess of black bile (in Greek, *melas* + *khole*) in the body.

As soon as you think physical substances in the body are responsible for emotions and behavior, biological interventions into love will appear viable. In the sixteenth and seventeenth centuries, physicians working with the theory of the four humors thought that "erotic love" was associated with the blood.[4] They believed that certain foods—white bread, eggs, and potatoes, for example—could help make one more "sanguine" (from *sanguis*, the Latin word for blood) and thus more "amorous." Being physically cooled down, on the other hand, was believed to suppress the blood and consequently any amorous tendencies.

In Sickness and in Health

Biological interventions have often focused on eliminating or "curing" love. Viewing love as something to "cure" requires first medicalizing it, which also has a long history. The idea of love as a source of severe physical and mental symptoms appears to go back as far as love itself, and in some eras "lovesickness" was treated very seriously as a medical condition.

We can contextualize the medicalization of love by considering the ancient Greek poet Sappho. She lived in the 600s BCE and arguably invented lyric love poetry—an art form that went on to play a huge role in shaping the composite image of romantic love. In her most famous poem, Sappho presents us with what appears to be a visceral description of passionate love and associated jealousy.[5] She describes the symptoms in detail: her heart flutters, she feels faint and feverish, she cannot see or speak, her ears thrum, she's dripping with sweat, she has the shakes, she's turning green—in fact, she's practically dying. (It turns out melodrama isn't a new invention either.)

Shakespeare also presented love as a serious illness. In Sonnet 147, for example, he uses explicit and protracted medical imagery to convey an experience of frustrated and despairing love, starting with "My love is as a fever longing still, / For that which longer nurseth the disease," before going on to say that his desire amounts to death, that his reason has left him, that his thoughts and words are "as madmen's are," and that he's "past cure." These sorts of sentiments were already sufficiently clichéd by 1885 for W. S. Gilbert to parody them in the libretto of *The Mikado*, in which Ko-Ko describes his "love" for Katisha as "a white-hot passion that is slowly but surely consuming my very vitals!"

Interestingly, while Shakespeare's Sonnet 147 sets out by presenting love as a physical illness (a "fever"), the metaphor then shifts to what we might now classify as a mental illness (a "madness"). But since his contemporaries would have construed both fevers and madness as imbalances in the four bodily humors, this distinction might have looked less significant to Shakespeare. Be that as it may, he is not at all subtle in developing the idea that love is a kind of insanity. His character Rosalind in *As You Like It* says, "Love is merely a madness, and, I tell you, deserves as well a dark house and a whip as madmen do: and the reason why they are not so punished and cured is, that the lunacy is so ordinary that the whippers are in love too." As this passage makes vivid, the association of love with mental illness can bring with it some really disturbing ideas about the latter.

Shakespeare wasn't the first to connect love with madness. In his *Phaedrus*, Plato has the character of Socrates describe *eros* as a form of madness (though here, as always, we should be wary of assuming that *eros* is the same thing as romantic love). Socrates initially dismisses *eros* as a distraction from the rational life. But he later apologizes for this, saying that *eros* can actually be a beneficial form of madness. He notes, though, that his opinions on this point "will not be believed by the merely clever, but will be accepted by the truly wise."[6]

In this statement-plus-retraction, and perhaps especially in this distinguishing of the "clever" from the "wise," Plato foreshadows the complex dance between love and rationality that has threaded throughout the subsequent history of thinking about love. It threads through this book too, in those early worries about "overthinking it," in Bertrand Russell's careful choice of words when advising future generations that "love is wise," and in the different ways love embeds itself in Enlightenment and Romantic conceptions of human nature. When presented as "madness," love is opposed to rationality—but maybe not to wisdom.

In any case, at your next dinner party you can challenge your friends to identify the one philosophical idea that unites the work of Plato, Shakespeare, Queen, and Beyoncé (the last two being responsible for the songs "Crazy Little Thing Called Love" and "Crazy in Love," respectively). The idea of love as madness is still very much with us, and throughout the ages it has served as one of the principal entry points for the medicalization of love.

Love Cures

Twentieth-century English professor Lawrence Babb, writing about the medicalization of love in its Renaissance incarnation, says, "In medical works, love is discussed as a brainsickness and is placed in company with madness, melancholy, hydrophobia, [and] frenzy."[7] He draws our attention to some passages in Renaissance works that explicitly medicalize love, including one from a sixteenth-century medical text by French physician André du Laurens. While agreeing with Robert Burton, author of the *Anatomy of Melancholy*, that "the last and best Cure of Love-Melancholy, is to let [the sufferers] have their Desire," du Laurens adds, "This course of cure being such, as neither ought nor can alwaies be put in practise, as being contrary vnto the lawes of God and men, we must haue recourse vnto . . . the industrie of the good Physition."[8]

The medical industry has always enthusiastically stepped up to the plate. In du Laurens's era, bloodletting was one proposed cure. Admittedly, this was medicine's proposed solution for pretty much everything at the time, but using it to cure love could make some kind of sense if you thought "amorousness" was due to a preponderance of blood unbalancing the four humors. Eating less food and keeping oneself busy were also recommended as cures for love-melancholy.

Babb reports that physicians of the Renaissance generally thought of love maladies as "a matter for grave concern." They proposed a mix of what we might now call therapeutic and biological interventions: "The former include mainly stratagems to divert the lover's mind from the beloved or to turn love into hatred or disgust; the latter, which may be used either as remedies or as preventives, include phlebotomy [i.e., bloodletting], drugs, exercise, and dietary schemes."

Just like direct biological interventions, therapeutic or behavioral interventions to "cure" love are both ancient and still with us. Ovid's poem "Remedia Amoris"—literally, "The Cure for Love"—is the Roman equivalent of an advice column for young men trying to get over women who are not interested in them. Don't bother with herbs or witchcraft, says Ovid. Try filling your time with law, warfare, hunting, and travel. "Love yields to business: be busy, and you will be safe."[9] He offers some dietary advice too, including an injunction to avoid onions—all kinds of onions, no matter where they come from, "be they Daunian or sent from Libyan shores or come they from Megara."

To understand the significance of all these ideas for "curing" love, we must identify the motivations, ideologies, and assumptions behind them. Ovid gives us valuable clues about what his contemporaries were thinking in trying to "cure" love. These ideas are still playing out in our own time: some of Ovid's advice wouldn't be out of place on the website of a contemporary "men's rights activist" or "pickup artist." For example, he urges men to "turn to the worse" anything that is attractive about a woman. And he offers examples of how to do this: "Call her fat, if she is full-breasted, black, if dark-complexioned; in a slender woman leanness can be made a reproach. If she is not simple, she can be called pert: if she is honest, she can be called simple." Ovid also recommends making women embarrass themselves by doing things they aren't good at: "Insist that she sing, if she be without a voice; make her dance, if she know not how to move her arms."

And he suggests showing up early in the morning before she's had time to get dressed properly so that the "hapless woman" can be let down "by her own defects."

Ovid may or may not have been attempting irony or parody. (Like Friedrich Nietzsche, he's sometimes given this kind of excuse.) Either way, the fact that he was writing thousands of years ago shines a light on how deeply unoriginal these attitudes to love and gender are. Even then, it made sense to think of love as a gendered war zone where the winner is the one who manages to feel and care the least. Of course, if that's what you think love is, then finding a "cure" will strike you as a winning strategy. I would suggest, though, that this is in fact an indication that something has gone wrong with your conception of love—and your worldview.

Disability and Addiction

Associating love with mental illness is one entry point for medicalizing love. There are at least two others: associating love with disability and with addiction.

Let's consider disability first. Perhaps the most common association under this heading is the idea that "love is blind." This is an instance of a broader pattern of metaphorical uses of blindness to capture a lack of awareness. This isn't always supposed to be a negative; justice is often depicted as blind to suggest unawareness of irrelevant distractions that could introduce bias. But "Love is blind" has the rather different connotation that when you are in love you are ignorant of—or "unable to see"—things like serious faults in your lover or the reasons why the relationship can never work out. As such, this application of the blindness metaphor trades on a harmful and inaccurate stereotype of blind people as ignorant or lacking awareness concerning important matters and making bad decisions ("stumbling into things") as a result.

We can salvage from the metaphor, without importing its discriminatory baggage, the idea that love often involves a lack of awareness. This can facilitate love's function: forming a nuclear bond is easier when you aren't noticing all of your lover's flaws. But it comes with the familiar problematic consequences, such as the misery and abuse that can result from committing (emotionally, financially, and so on) without adequate awareness of who your partner really is.

Like its associations with blindness and mental illness, love's association with addiction is so well established as to be a cliché. Robert Palmer famously rocked out about love addiction in his 1980s hit "Addicted to Love," listing its various symptoms in a manner reminiscent of Sappho's 2,500-year-old poem. But we are now learning that there are real physical and neurochemical similarities between some kinds of love and some kinds of chemical addiction.

In a collaborative 2010 paper, neuroscientist Lucy Brown highlights some of these similarities.[10] She reports her research (undertaken with others, including Helen Fisher) on the brains of young adults recently rejected in love, "arguably the group showing the greatest 'addiction' to another person." These studies found that in such subjects the ventral tegmental area (part of the brain's "reward system" associated with dopamine production and distribution) showed greater activation, a phenomenon also often seen in the early stages of romantic love. This suggests that "the sight of the sweetheart is still rewarding" after rejection. However, more disturbingly, the recently rejected subjects also displayed patterns of heightened activity in certain regions of the brain previously found to correlate with craving in cocaine addicts.

We've come a long way from the idea that love-melancholy stems from an excess of blood, but in many ways we are still engaged in the same project. Drawing on advances in neuroscience, ethicists are beginning to discuss the real possibility of bringing love within the scope of modern drug treatments. The association with addiction is particularly foregrounded here, the idea being that it may be possible to "cure" love using methods already used to treat addiction and/or to develop new treatments based on love's similarities with addiction. For example, ethicists have suggested that "just as heroin addicts are sometimes given oral naltrexone to block the pharmacological effects of their drug, we could use oxytocin antagonists to reduce the reward an individual receives from being close to another person."[11]

Real Drugs . . . Real Love?

Maybe we are about to hit the moment when "curing love" with drugs is no longer just fiction or quackery. It might, however, still be grounded in confusion. Is it really love we are trying to cure?

I can see why we might want to cure things like infatuation, obsession, stalking, or intimate partner abuse. But these aren't love. In fact, calling them that is dangerous. The word "love" is powerful and typically interpreted as very positive. Deploying that word can effectively conceal what is actually a terrible situation. The violence of an abusive partner, for example, is not the result of "too much love." But abusers call it that to gain sympathy and keep themselves in a position to cause further harm.

It is perhaps more controversial whether the kind of attachment that makes it hard for an abused partner to leave a toxic relationship is a kind of "love" that needs to be "cured." But in many such cases, the experience may not be one of genuine love at all: it could indicate an unhealthy dependence, a fear of leaving, or a suite of other things. Even if love is present, it's not clear that the love itself needs curing (as opposed to the effects of trauma, a lack of personal safety or autonomy as a result of the abuser's actions, and so on).

The best way to approach the problems created by obsession and abuse is not to talk about "curing love" but to draw a clear distinction between love and the things that are causing harm and need to be "cured." bell hooks's work on love has inspired this strategy, which is, to my mind, the only one that will enable us to tackle the real problems with sufficient clarity. Talk of "curing love" only serves to muddy the waters—the last thing we need in such difficult situations.

We should also bear in mind that we have a history of attempting to "cure" certain forms of love and that history hardly inspires confidence. The devastating effects of attempts to "cure" queer people's romantic feelings and orientations using "chemical castration" and "conversion therapy" are well-known. Our track record is not a shining example of humanity's ability to wield medical technologies with competence and compassion.

What about the idea of using drugs to induce or sustain love? This may sound less alarming, on the face of it, than "curing" love. But again, we will do well to take a careful look at the motivations before we sign up too enthusiastically. A recent argument for chemically induced love claimed that "marriage is good for children especially if it is happy," the idea being that using drugs to keep married couples in love, and hence together, would be beneficial.[12] But are we to assume that a particular subset of marriages—the ones that would have broken up if not for chemical intervention—are also "good for children"? I don't know what evidence we could have for such a claim, but in the absence of evidence, it is suspicious.

Even more revealingly, the authors of this argument also offer another, which they say is based on justice. They write, "Currently, the natural lottery creates inequality. Some men are successful and some women are attractive, having the widest choice of mates. Others are less desirable. Chemically inducing lust and attractiveness might give those lower on the tree of life a chance to climb higher. This could create a more level playing field."

By now, you should be well placed to identify some familiar ideology at work here. For example, there are standard gender stereotypes: notice the assumption, without comment, that the widest choice of mates goes to the attractive women and the successful men. Most important, though, is the suggestion that we view the ethics of love and sex through the lens of equitable distribution, or justice. We need to remember that we are talking about people and their most intimate relationships with other people. Is the idea that the unattractive women will voluntarily choose to take drugs in order to become available to the unsuccessful men (and vice versa)? Or will they be forced to take such drugs? The first option sounds bizarre, but the second is disturbing. Anyhow, who decides who counts as unattractive or unsuccessful in the first place? In such subjective assessments, whose standards are we to take as definitive?

Let's drill down a bit deeper to see what's gone wrong. We've already come across the big picture idea at work behind the scenes in the "justice" argument: the notion that romantic partners are a kind of resource akin to wealth or private property. This idea is manifest here in the use of language like "competition" and "lottery" to describe what is in reality a search for intimacy and loving connection, as well as in the presentation of free romantic choice as a source of inequality that we should rectify with redistributive measures.

The idea of partners as resources or property is a cultural hangover: a remnant of monogamy's origins in the possession and control of women as a route to assured paternity and the inheritance of a man's wealth by his biological children. This model viewed women as something akin to livestock or brood mares. Extending this horrifying attitude to romantic partners in general is not progress; I have no patience with the equation of people with property. That idea's time has well and truly passed (and should never have arrived). As a philosopher and a human, I am drawn to what the future of romantic love might look like if we could just stop thinking about other people—including our romantic partners—as property or prizes, as things we can win or possess, or as things it makes sense to redistribute in the name of "justice."

I believe we can eradicate that mind-set. But it will take a shift in attitudes—a big one—and we can't achieve this by medicating people.

Then again, such a shift isn't going to happen anytime soon, and individuals are suffering right now because of love—or at least because of experiences they're calling "love." If we can help them with drugs, we should, right? The short answer is, of course, yes. We should help people if we can. But the long answer is that, as with any medical intervention, we must approach this possibility with an eye to the grave risks of papering over symptoms while the real issues go unaddressed. And we should be extremely careful about how we describe what we're doing. We should hear alarm bells when intervening medically in an abusive relationship gets described as "curing love."

Nor should we get carried away with the idea that we really can cure any or all problematic symptoms with drugs. The relevant neuroscience is still in its infancy. We have advanced considerably beyond the theory of the four humors, but it's still a good bet that any drug interventions we propose today will, in a few hundred years, sound about as helpful as opening a vein to make someone less sanguine or as effective as Ovid's ban on onions.

One of the safest predictions you can make about our future is that it will resemble our past and present. It takes highly sophisticated weather-forecasting technology to outperform the algorithm that says tomorrow will be like today. But as we improve our understanding of the biology of love, keeping love's dual nature in mind just might help us avoid repeating past patterns of medicalizing and individualizing issues that are truly neither medical nor individual. We need to be aware that love's biology—and, more generally, love at the level of the individual—is only part of the picture. It's not the only place, or even the most obvious place, to seek a diagnosis when things go wrong. If something is seriously wrong with the social role of romantic love, drugs will not fix it—even, or perhaps especially, if they work.

Despite what the romantic mystique would have us believe, we can change the nature of love. We can certainly rewrite the social script. We may also be able to retrain the biological actor. And this means we have some serious thinking to do about which of these options we want to pursue, and how, and, crucially, why. As we move into a period of increased understanding of the biology of love, the attendant ethical risks and responsibilities will only keep growing. We will need to think harder about this than we've ever had to before.

The One Weird Trick for a Fabulous Love Life

As much as our understanding of the science of love is improving, it is important to approach all the sensationalizing headlines about it with one eyebrow pre-raised. "Scientists can now tell if you're in love by scanning your brain," ran one recent headline on the website *Science Alert*, "and they know if you're faking it."[13] They know? Oh, you're so busted.

Except, of course, you're not. Headlines in this style are like the images on the outside of a microwave meal or the title I chose for this section: if you base your expectations on such unrealistic promises, you will be disappointed. Here's what the scientists who did the work behind that headline actually said: "The results shed light on the underlying neural mechanisms of romantic love, and demonstrate the possibility of applying a resting-state fMRI approach for investigating romantic love."[14] They found some statistical correlations, among a group of college students, between brain scan results and being "currently intensely in love" (as measured by a rather problematic questionnaire designed in the 1980s).[15] This is quite a limited finding and certainly does not mean they can "tell" who is or isn't in love just by scanning brains. They cannot prove you're "faking it," and they are not coming after you to take away your love credentials.

Staying alert to what we are really learning also means remembering that every conversation about love—be it scientific, medical, or anything else—comes with masses of baggage in the form of preconfigured social attitudes and expectations. Neglecting this leaves everyone vulnerable—particularly groups excluded or harmed by the current social script for romantic love and those experiencing abuse in love's name. But it's risky for anyone to make major life decisions based on love without understanding what love is and where our assumptions about it really come from.

We are similarly vulnerable in deciding whether to pursue options for medical intervention. To make these choices in a responsible way, a good first step is to see romantic love as in a state of continual interplay between the biological and the social. Whatever else the future holds, as long as we retain our own dual natures as biological and social beings, love will have a foot in both camps as well. No pill will cure the problems we have built into love's social role, but we may be able to manipulate the biology of love more wisely once we appreciate this.

As the Serenity Prayer suggests, we need courage to change the things we can and serenity to accept the things we cannot. But when it comes to the future of love, we most urgently need wisdom—not just to know what we can and cannot change, but to know what kind of creature we are dealing with in the first place, to locate the hidden seams between love's biological machinery and its ideological contours, and to see clearly the motivations behind proposed interventions. Acquiescence in the romantic mystique—the idea that we can't change anything about love and thus don't have to try—represents a dearth of courage and an excess of serenity. But overenthusiasm about the medical manipulation of love is not exactly the inverse (an excess of courage and a dearth of serenity). Rather, it is symptomatic of a deep lack of wisdom: a misconstrual of the nature of the beast.

Coda:
Make It So

*They say the owl was a baker's daughter. Lord, we know
what we are, but know not what we may be.*

—William Shakespeare, *Hamlet*

Love's Politics

Say anything about changing or challenging romantic love, and
some people are going to hear you as advocating for a world
where love has been eliminated and replaced by constant, guilt-
free sex. That's a weird leap of logic when you think about it.
Where does it come from?

One piece of the puzzle is that sex and love have been assimi-
lated into a political divide and set in opposition. Roughly speaking, advocating for sex is viewed as progressive or liberal, while
advocating for love is viewed as traditionalist or conservative.

This manifests in many ways—for example, when people try to make a relationship sound less respectable by saying it's "just sex" or, conversely, make it sound more respectable by saying it's "true love." The crucial fixed point in these discussions is that love itself is respectable, reliable, sensible, dependable, and lots of other things that conservatives like.

Two mistakes are happening here. First, love and sex are not in any kind of opposition. They are not the same thing, but they're not competitors either.[1] Second, love is far too powerful to cede to any one political ideology. In reality, there is nothing conservative about love per se: it has been a site of radical social change, just as it has been a site of stability and tradition. Love wasn't busy being respectable in the 1960s; it was wild and free.

Changing the social role of romantic love is never easy, but love's politicization as a force for conservatism makes it all the more challenging. While I can't predict the future any more than you can, we can probably all take a lesson from weather forecasting: by and large, tomorrow will be like today. Any change will happen incrementally and against a background of continuity. I do, however, have a guess as to which incremental change is coming next. One norm structuring love's social role has been gradually coming under more and more pressure, to the point where it has become obviously unsustainable. I think the next change will have to be one that relieves this pressure.

The problematic norm is that everyone should have one true love forever, with the important corollaries that (1) this entails sexual monogamy forever, and (2) it should be enforced for men as well as for women. It's not hard to see that a huge head of steam has built up behind that idea. High and rising divorce rates suggest that the one-true-love-forever model is not sustainable as a universal norm. And the idea that one will eventually and inevitably lose sexual and/or romantic interest in one's long-term partner has become so normalized as to be a rom com trope in its own right. Relationship therapist Esther Perel puts it this way: "Everywhere romanticism has entered, there seems to be a crisis of desire."[2] Yet, at the moment, we seem to be attempting to treat this problem at the individual level: with medical interventions like Viagra, with couples therapy, and with forlorn purchases of exciting lingerie.

We can go back to philosopher Bertrand Russell for some perspective on all this. Russell thought that society had shut down women's sexuality as a way of controlling paternity: it assured men that wives would not desire any other man but would still be duty-bound to submit sexually to their spouses. However, this strategy doesn't work once women are socially and legally empowered to refuse sex within marriage. Marital rape was still legal in some parts of the United States until 1993 and in England until 1991, and change in practice arrives at an even more glacial pace than change in principle. When you think about it, then, we are only just tumbling to the consequences of the old strategy's expiration. We are now scrambling for a new one.

It is no coincidence that we are just now seeing a new drug, Flibanserin, marketed as a treatment for "female sexual dysfunction," approved for use in the United States. Originally developed as an antidepressant, the drug wasn't found sufficiently effective. Its effectiveness for increasing female sexual desire is also quite limited, and there are potentially serious side effects. (Flibanserin was rejected for FDA approval twice before being accepted.) But desperate times call for desperate measures. And the universal one-true-love-forever model has so far outstayed its welcome that we are, as a society, getting pretty desperate.

Tomorrow Could Be Like Yesterday

Even if medical interventions can help some people, they are not enough to suppress a problem on this scale. They are a patch: an attempt to paper over the symptoms of a social problem by "treating" individuals. The attitudes behind Flibanserin are reminiscent of the mass deployment of tranquilizers in the 1960s to quell women's dissatisfaction with the romantic gender role of housewife, a phenomenon immortalized in the Rolling Stones song "Mother's Little Helper." As we continue to live longer, demand personal satisfaction from romantic relationships, and— crucially—exercise the right to refuse sex even if we are married and female, the pressure on the one-true-love-forever model continues to intensify.

Once we identify romantic love as a dual-natured phenomenon, we have a powerful way of understanding what is happening and what our options are. We can diagnose a case of unsustainably poor casting: a large-scale mismatch between the ancient biological machinery of love (the actor from my earlier analogy) and the modern social role that it is now expected to play. The social script still prescribes a one-true-love-forever model but now with two added features: greater sexual autonomy for women and enforced sexual monogamy for men. And the biological actor in many of us is simply a terrible casting choice for this role. I don't doubt that for some people it is a good fit, but there are just far too many for whom it is not.

This wouldn't be the first time such poor casting has eventually become unsustainable. The exclusion of same-sex relationships from the social role of romantic love couldn't, and didn't, switch off queer people's neurochemical love responses to same-sex partners. Attempts to retrain the biological actor by "treating" queer individuals have failed spectacularly. The solution was to rewrite the script for romantic love at the social level. Thankfully, this approach is now winning out in the part of the world where I live.

In the same way, society's insistence on the one-true-love-forever model can't, and won't, shut down the neurochemistry of all the people who fall in love with a new person after promising themselves to an existing partner or of all the people who grow bored of long-term monogamous romance with their spouses. We can keep trying to retrain the biological actor by diagnosing these individuals with a medical problem and attempting to "cure" their desire for others or their chronic boredom. Or we can reconsider the failing social norm.

Recent work by ethicists Brian Earp, Anders Sandberg, and Julian Savulescu has identified options approximately resembling these two.[3] Like many others in this business, they lean toward efforts to prop up lifelong monogamy with biological interventions. They say, "We know that adultery causes harm," and so does divorce. Their list of what "we know" continues: "The emotional harm associated with adultery is built in through jealousy . . . designed to keep parental resources focused on existing offspring. Jealousy, then, as opposed to adultery, is consistent with values aimed at keeping families intact." As Bertrand Russell noted in *Marriage and Morals*, "Jealousy has the sanction of moralists." This is as true now as it was in the 1920s. Notice, too, how terms like "built in" and "designed" are used to hint that a kind of biological determinism underwrites the envisaged family values.

Earp and his coauthors further argue that "a hands off adultery norm might also raise concerns about equity, since men are much more likely than women to desire extramarital sex. . . . Finally, convincing 97% of the population to reverse a cornerstone social value seems unlikely, to say the least." They think all this is grounds to conclude that "the norm against adultery is probably worth retaining on a broad scale—however 'unnatural' absolute sexual fidelity may in fact be."

All those claims about what "we know" might resonate with the authors' own experiences, but your mileage may vary. Mine has. In fact, the argument has many problems, several of which we've already addressed in other contexts. For example, this trope of appealing to equity is probably starting to sound familiar by now. In this incarnation, it's phrased as a concern that if nonmonogamy is tolerated, it will be harder for men than for women to get as much extramarital sex as they want, and that wouldn't be fair to men. (We are left to wonder how equitable the current arrangement is for women.) The underlying assumption is that relationships are the sort of thing where it makes sense to think in terms of equitable distribution. But, on pain of sounding like a broken record, they aren't. Love, sex, and people are not property or resources that we get to manage and distribute in the name of "equity." Men are not entitled to demand a "fair share" of love, sex, or women.

We can also think back to earlier discussions of how contemporary empirical research is raising doubts about the gender stereotype—assumed without comment in the above argument—that women want monogamy and don't want sex except with their spouses. And we might recall Russell's suggestion that it is preferable to rein in jealousy rather than love.

But there is a new point to make here as well, and it concerns one of the most alarming assumptions in the argument: the idea that, if we are unlikely to convince 97 percent of the population to reverse a cornerstone social value, that means the norm is probably worth retaining. Russell is once more a source of inspiration when facing an argument like this. As he said, "The fact that an opinion has been widely held is no evidence whatever that it is not utterly absurd."

Let's not forget that as recently as 1958, another cornerstone social value prohibited interracial love in the United States. At that time, 94 percent of Americans disapproved of "marriages between white and coloured people."[4] We could have reasoned that it was unlikely, to say the least, that we could change this. We could have wielded that as a reason to conclude that the norms against interracial relationships were probably worth retaining.

I'm glad we didn't.

'Til Expiration Dates Do Us Part

Over the last century, the contours of love's social profile have changed quite a lot. Romantic love is no longer strictly limited to opposite-sex love or to love between two people of the same race.

As the one-true-love-forever model now fails us, will we soon remove the monogamy and permanence restrictions as well?

My bet is no. We are not going to remove both these features from the composite image of romantic love anytime soon. That's too big a change to accomplish all at once. Instead, I wager that one of these features is about to give, as a sort of safety valve that will permit the preservation of the other, at least for a time. I actually predict that the "forever" part will give way first.

Many people around me are already comfortable with the idea of serial temporary monogamy. While you're still not exactly supposed to plan for it, de facto serial temporary monogamy is no longer scandalous or even surprising. Given this starting point, chosen—and eventually de jure—temporary monogamy looks like a relative shoo-in. Over the protests of traditionalists,[5] many marrying couples are already choosing to replace "till death us do part" with alternatives like "as long as love lasts" or are simply omitting to mention the issue of duration altogether in their vows. Many are making prenuptial agreements to determine what will happen if and when the marriage ends.

Philosopher Daniel Nolan has recently advocated for legal temporary marriage on grounds of fairness.[6] He argues that straightforward considerations of marriage equality should extend to those who want a temporary marriage. He also points out that some religious and cultural traditions include temporary marriage forms, which means that a legal system that fails to accommodate them privileges certain religious and cultural traditions over others.

The introduction of temporary monogamous marriage would relieve the pressure behind the one-true-love-forever model while allowing for broad continuity with the current status quo. And gradual change against a backdrop of continuity is how these things work. Romantic gender stereotypes, monogamy, nuclear privilege, and so on, can all be preserved in a social structure where some marriages have a prearranged end date. We could even preserve stability with regard to raising children if we treated their arrival as automatically transforming a marriage from a temporary one into a permanent one (as Bertrand Russell suggested back in 1929), or at least into one that lasts until the children reach adulthood. Perhaps most significantly, from an ideological standpoint, we can retain the deep implicit connections between romantic love and private property: we need only reconceptualize marriage as renting rather than purchasing.

In all these ways, temporary monogamy, while it might sound a little unromantic at the moment, poses far less of a threat to the social role of romantic love than polyamory does. Polyamory directly challenges two often invisible (but ideologically precious) ideas: paternity control through the sexual restriction of women and the conception of a romantic partner as one's private property. It strikes at the heart of the historical purpose of romantic love (and also, in my opinion, at the heart of what is wrong with it today). Perhaps not unrelatedly, while both polyamory and temporary marriage are anathema to religious and social conservatives, only polyamory currently induces disgust responses from across the entire spectrum of political orientation. These days, if you have two temporary relationships sequentially, you are normal. If you have two permanent relationships simultaneously, you are "a degenerate herpes-infested whore."[7]

While I hope that polyamory can gradually become less illegal in places like the United States—where legislatures could take outmoded adultery laws off the books without any tangible effect—and that those in nonmonogamous relationships can move toward some minimal formal protection from discrimination, I predict that polyamory will continue to be punishable by death in many parts of the world and that people like me will continue to be regarded as disgusting and sinful by many of our neighbors for the foreseeable future.

Are We Unstoppable?

I believe we can, collectively, effect unimaginable changes to romantic love's social role. But just how far could these changes be taken? How much can we mess about with romantic love before we have destroyed it?

Let's tackle this possibility head-on. What if we did destroy romantic love? Does it matter? Maybe we should replace romantic love with other kinds of love, free from the unfortunate baggage. Romantic love has always been intimately connected with the idea that people—especially women—are a kind of private property. It has been a powerful tool in the enforcement of class structures, racist segregation, and homophobic oppression. Are we sure we want to keep it around?

While this is an intriguing question, it's moot as far as planning goes. I don't think it is feasible to abolish romantic love, at least not until we live in the kind of science fiction future where we can replace or reprogram our meat brains. We could try to tear up the social script for romantic love: to stop organizing our social lives around it, stop talking about it as if it were a desirable thing, and perhaps even stop talking about it as if it were a thing at all. But I think it's pretty clear that the results of such an attempt would be suppression, secrecy, suffering, and/or constant medical intervention to maintain the brave new status quo. If we tore up love's social script, the ancient biological machinery of love would persist, and it would insist. In fact it's hard to see this future as anything but a science fiction dystopia.[8]

Another possible future sees us destroying romantic love at the social level in a very different way. Instead of forbidding or suppressing it, we just keep broadening the social role of love until it no longer imposes any substantive constraints. By that point, romantic love is no longer a distinctive thing, because pretty much any and every kind of vaguely positive feeling toward something or someone else counts as romantic love. Is that a viable future? Could we gradually replace all of love's traditional characterizing features—monogamy, permanence, heteroromanticism, romantic gender roles, and so on—over time? Would there still be romantic love at the end of that process?

While this is probably more feasible than suppression, in practice I suspect the question is again ultimately moot. Romantic love is not going to undergo a total replacement of all of its characteristic features. It's true that many recent changes to the social role of love have tended toward making love less restrictive, but the biological machinery of love will continue to serve as an anchor for the kind of social script writing that has any realistic chance of working out. Unless we get a lot better at neuroscience, love is going to retain its recognizable biological symptoms. Racing hearts and the feeling of dopamine reward will be a part of the picture, as long as there are hearts and dopamine. As long as there is oxytocin, there will be cases of the warm fuzzies. Any social script for love that gave us no way to make coherent sense of these experiences would just land us with another case of unsustainably poor casting.

I think we are capable of striking the necessary balance: changing what needs to change without destroying romantic love entirely. Here's how. Romantic love, at the social level, could have the function of taking as input attraction and affection between adults (not necessarily a particular number or of particular genders) and outputting intimate bonds and relationships that are special and significant in people's lives. Optional add-ons can then include sex, kids, home building, family building, agreeing not to enter into other relationships, caring for a dog together, writing love poems . . . whatever floats the boat of the people in the boat. These optional extras would work like a buffet: people would be free to decide on the features they wanted in their own relationships without facing stigma for what they did or didn't choose. And they would be free to switch it up over time, going back to the buffet to add something new to their plates or remove something they didn't like. We would ditch the idea of a "standard model" for how romantic love should look.

Might it then become impossible to distinguish romantic love from other kinds of love, such as the love in an intense friendship? I don't see that this would be a common problem; often a selection of the optional extras would be present, helping to determine that the love involved is romantic. But in an ideal world—where we have ceased privileging romantic love as the norm for everybody—*who cares*? If it's a close call whether a relationship is romantic or platonic, the people in the relationship could just call it how they want it. Why not?

Choose Your Own Adventure

When asked what messages he would send to future generations, Bertrand Russell picked two. One we've already encountered: "Love is wise, hatred is foolish." The other was this: "When you are studying any matter, or considering any philosophy, ask yourself only what are the facts and what is the truth that the facts bear out. Never let yourself be diverted either by what you wish to believe or by what you think would have beneficent social effects if it were believed."

I wish I could believe that polyamorous relationships like mine will soon be widely socially acknowledged as genuine and normal cases of romantic love. But I don't. I also think that a general belief that romantic love has no biology and is a pure social construct would have beneficent social effects—at least in the short term. This would help us feel more empowered to make changes to love's social role without feeling constrained by (what we take to be) our biology. But the truth is that love has a biological nature too, and in the long run we ignore this at our peril.

Yet the truth of love's dual nature is empowering in its own right. It empowers us to seek out genuinely possible changes to love's social role, without neglecting or dismissing the fact that we have the biology we do. It means we can respect love's biological nature without simply regarding ourselves as love-driven automata at the mercy of our brain chemistry or evolutionary history. We can talk about what it means for love's biology and its social role to be mismatched and how we might address those mismatches responsibly. The dual-nature theory also shows why the humanities, the social sciences, and the natural sciences will all play crucial roles in coming to a full understanding of what love is and how these enterprises can collaborate rather than compete for ownership of love as a subject matter.

On a personal level, understanding love's dual nature can contextualize our own experiences with love. We come to see our individual stories as embedded within social structures that we didn't choose, any more than we chose the biology that drives us. The dual-nature theory reveals how romantic love points both within and beyond the privacy of our own heads, hearts, homes, and relationships. In so doing it empowers those of us who don't conform to the "script" to resist the message that we are doing it wrong: we can turn the tables and question the script itself. And, crucially, it shows us how to do this without being antiscience or denying that the biology of love is real and important. This makes our challenges harder to write off.

The script is an off-the-peg deal: sex, passion, affection, care, commitment, settling down, marriage, earning less or more than your spouse, doing more or less of the housework, having kids, getting bored with sex, monogamy forever, then death. And it comes with a side order of amatonormativity, designed to make it an offer you can't refuse: it's this or a life of loneliness (according to US Supreme Court Justice Anthony Kennedy).

We can collectively change this script, alter the emergent contours in our composite image of love. That takes time, of course. But at an individual level we can start customizing right now: start designing for ourselves instead of accepting the off-the-peg model for love (and life). We can custom-build any new relationship from the ground up, philosophically and reflectively. And we can approach any existing relationship the same way, because it is an ongoing project: like a living thing, it grows and changes. In fact, every life is like that, whether it includes romantic relationships or not. It doesn't matter whether, in the past, you've followed the script without even noticing. You deserve to choose your own adventure now.

That said, defying the script can be hard, and the costs of doing so fall on the "rebels." Not everyone is in a position to absorb those costs, which makes it all the more important for those of us who can to speak up and be heard. When we challenge assumptions and openly customize our relationships, the benefits accrue to everybody, rebel or not. We all gain a conceptual space in which to step back and ask ourselves which—if any—aspects of the preexisting script for love we want to mix and match into our own lives. Even those who like a traditional flavor of relationship get to choose it rather than having it handed to them, and this exercise of conscious choice makes such relationships more comfortable, stable, healthy, and admirable.

Nonconformity can change the world. I mean this literally: if we start customizing, the composite image of love will change. Love's new contours will emerge, and they might surprise us. In this book I've made some predictions for the future; it's been fun guessing what's going to happen, and it'll be fun waiting around to be proven wrong. But I hope it's obvious that my guesswork doesn't matter. What matters is what we create. Whatever happens, we will make it so.

You are part of that. So if I had to whittle this book down to one message, it would be a simple one: *think about love for yourself.* Do not buy it when people tell you to stop "overthinking" love. It is not an exaggeration to say that love can matter as much as life itself: for love, some people will give up their homes, their families, their jobs, their aspirations, and everything else—even their lives. And yet so much is going on behind the scenes that affects us all. We need to uncover that hidden machinery and not turn away when it gets ugly, which it sometimes does. Once we do, we'll discover that—in all sorts of ways—we ourselves are the "man behind the curtain." We're the ones running this show. Our decisions about love's social script and the biological interventions we might one day develop shape what love is and what it could be.

These are not decisions to be entered into unadvisedly or lightly, but reverently, discreetly, advisedly, soberly. Or, at the very least, with some minimal awareness of what a huge thing we are doing. Romantic love cannot continue to be something we just stumble into and accept. That goes for the love in individual lives, but it goes equally for the bigger picture: the collective script we are writing together. We deserve to know what our options really are. It's time we got to choose our own adventures.

What do you want from yours?

Acknowledgments

I am lucky to have an amazing support system around me. That is what makes things like this book possible.

Thanks to my research assistants Jasper Heaton and Aida Roige, to my directed-study student Jelena Markovic, and to the students in the philosophy majors' seminar on the metaphysics of romantic love at the University of British Columbia during the 2014–2015 academic year, who helped me think about these topics.

Thanks to the Hampton Fund at the University of British Columbia and the Social Sciences and Humanities Research Council of Canada for their financial support of my research on the nature of love.

Thanks to early readers Liam Kofi Bright, Richard Heck, Daniel Nolan, Kathryn Pogin, and Audrey Yap for valuable comments and feedback on drafts. Especial thanks to Jonathan Jenkins Ichikawa for reading and commenting on the whole thing and to Ray Hsu for help with manuscript editing and for sharing his writerly expertise with a newbie.

Thanks to all the philosophers who didn't tell me I was doing it wrong for working on this book and to all the philosophers working to challenge philosophy's narrow self-conception and make space for something greater.

Thanks to Marina Adshade and Mandy Len Catron, fellow members of the Vancouver Love Triangle, for conversations and camaraderie.

Thanks to Quynh Do and T. J. Kelleher at Basic Books and Martha Webb at the McDermid Agency for their support and guidance through the process of writing and publishing.

Thanks to Matchstick on Fraser for the coffee and ambience that fueled the creation of most of the initial manuscript.

Thanks to my inspiring and wonderful family and friends. Especial thanks to my dog, Mezzo, who provided emotional support, made sure I went outside every day, and listened patiently to my ideas even though she herself has never been particularly interested in the philosophy of romantic love.

Above all, thanks to my lovers, past and present, without whom I personally would not have the first clue about any of this stuff. Or indeed most other things.

Notes

Notes to Prologue

1. One example can be found in philosopher Alan Soble's article "The Unity of Romantic Love," *Philosophy and Theology* 1, no. 4 (1987): 374–397. For more about how and why philosophers build monogamy assumptions into their theories of love, see Carrie Jenkins, "Modal Monogamy," *Ergo* 2, no. 8 (2015): 175–194.

2. Savage talked about this change of heart in 2014: Dan Savage, "SL Letter of the Day: Happy Anniversary," *Savage Love* (blog), *Stranger*, August 14, 2014, http://slog.thestranger.com/slog/archives/2014/08/14/sl-letter-of-the-day-happy-anniversary.

3. See, e.g., Benoit Monin and Dale T. Miller, "Moral Credentials and the Expression of Prejudice," *Journal of Personality and Social Psychology* 81, no. 1 (2001): 33–43.

Notes to Introduction

1. This wording is from *Plato's Theory of Knowledge: The Theaetetus and The Sophist*, trans. Francis Cornford (New York: Liberal Arts Press, 1957), available at Archive.org, https://archive.org/stream/theaetetus00plat/theaetetus00plat_djvu.txt.

2. December 29, 2015.

3. From Simon Rich, *The Last Girlfriend on Earth and Other Love Stories* (New York: Little, Brown & Co., 2013).

4. See, e.g., "What Is Love?," *Economist*, December 17, 2008, http://www.economist.com/node/12800025; Jim Al-Khalili et al., "What Is Love? Five Theories on the Greatest Emotion of All," *Guardian*, December 13, 2012, http://www.theguardian.com/commentisfree/2012/dec/13/what-is-love-five-theories.

5. bell hooks, *All About Love: New Visions* (New York: William Morrow, 2000).

6. Betty Friedan, *The Feminine Mystique* (New York: W. W. Norton & Co., 1963).

7. John Shand, "Love as If," *Essays in Philosophy* 12, no. 1 (2011): 4–17, http://commons.pacificu.edu/eip/vol12/iss1/2.

Notes to Chapter 1

1. Keats is concerned with the loss of magic in nature generally, not in love per se. It's interesting to note that as its mysteries are praised, nature is feminized as a "mother," exemplifying what would later be identified as the *feminine mystique*. Keats's rainbow is also presented as feminine (a gender decision with a venerable history: in ancient Greek mythology, the goddess Iris was associated with the rainbow).

2. In "Some Remarks on Humor," preface to *A Subtreasury of American Humor*, ed. E. B. White and Katherine S. White (New York: Coward-McCann, 1941.)

3. Christopher Ryan and Cacilda Jethá discuss such models in chapters 6 and 7 of *Sex at Dawn: The Prehistoric Origins of Modern Sexuality* (New York: Harper, 2010).

4. Helen Fisher, *Why We Love: The Nature and Chemistry of Romantic Love* (New York: Henry Holt & Co., 2004).

5. See Donatella Marazziti and Domenico Canale, "Hormonal Changes When Falling in Love," *Psychoneuroendocrinology* 29, no. 7 (August 2004): 931–936. Interestingly, this study also looked at testosterone, finding that it tends to increase in women and decrease in men during the early stages of love.

6. The philosophy nerd in me is actually interested in discussing this issue at great length but will save it for another occasion.

7. See Robert Nozick, "Love's Bond," in *The Examined Life: Philosophical Meditations* (New York: Simon and Schuster, 1989).

8. I recently taught a seminar on romantic love, and several of my students reported that something felt right about Nozick's theory.

9. Julian Savulescu and Anders Sandberg, "Neuroenhancement of Love and Marriage: The Chemicals Between Us," *Neuroethics* 1, no. 1 (March 2008): 31–44.

10. Brian D. Earp et al., "If I Could Just Stop Loving You: Antilove Biotechnology and the Ethics of a Chemical Breakup," *American Journal of Bioethics* 13, no. 11 (2013): 3–17.

11. See Hui Wang et al., "Histone Deacetylase Inhibitors Facilitate Partner Preference Formation in Female Prairie Voles," *Nature Neuroscience* 16 (2013): 919–924.

12. Sven Nyholm considers this question in "Love Troubles: Human Attachment and Biomedical Enhancements," *Journal of Applied Philosophy* 32, no. 2 (May 2015): 190–202.

13. See K. D. O'Leary et al., "Is Long-Term Love More Than a Rare Phenomenon? If So, What Are Its Correlates?," *Social Psychology and Personality Science* 3 (2012): 241–249.

14. See Bianca Acevedo et al. (including Fisher), "Neural Correlates of Long-Term Intense Romantic Love," *Social Cognitive and Affective Neuroscience* (2011).

15. Helen Fisher, "The Brain in Love," TED, February 2008, https://www.ted.com/talks/helen_fisher_studies_the_brain_in_love.

16. I discuss these issues in Carrie Jenkins, "Knowing Our Own Hearts: Self-Reporting and the Science of Love," forthcoming in *Philosophical Issues*.

Notes to Chapter 2

1. A study found that subjects rated one and the same smell significantly worse when it was labeled "body odor" than when it was labeled "cheddar cheese." The results are reported in Ivan de Araujo et al., "Cognitive Modulation of Olfactory Processing," *Neuron* 46, no. 4 (May 2005): 671–679.

2. Anne Beall and Robert Sternberg, "The Social Construction of Love," *Journal of Social and Personal Relationships* 12, no. 3 (August 1995): 417–438.

3. Williams Jankoviak and Edward Fischer, "A Cross-Cultural Perspective on Romantic Love," *Ethnology* 31, no. 2 (April 1992): 149–155.

4. Margaret Wente, "Race and Gender: I Feel Therefore I Am," *Globe and Mail*, June 19, 2015. The article may be read in full at http://www.theglobeandmail.com/globe-debate/race-and-gender-i-feel-therefore-i-am/article25039792, though I cannot say I recommend it.

5. I am repurposing the phrase. It has been used by other writers—notably Scott Peck and bell hooks—with a different meaning. They had in mind that we should think of love as being a matter of how someone acts: what they do rather than just how they feel on the inside. My focus here is different: I am focusing on what love does at the societal level (as opposed to what individuals do when they are in love).

6. This list of features partly overlaps with (and is inspired by) the features of genuine love identified by bell hooks in *All About Love: New Visions* (New York: William Morrow, 2000). One important thing about this list is that it directs attention toward features of love that are not all about *feeling* a certain way. This forms an important part of hooks's argument that abusive relationships are not loving: abusive individuals' merely feeling like they love their victims does not mean that they actually do.

Notes to Chapter 3

1. Anders Österling, Permanent Secretary of the Swedish Academy, "Award Ceremony Speech," Nobelprize.org, 1950, http://www.nobelprize.org/nobel_prizes/literature/laureates/1950/press.html.

2. Bertrand Russell, *Marriage and Morals* (New York: Liveright, 1929).

3. Christopher Ryan and Cacilda Jethá, *Sex at Dawn: The Prehistoric Origins of Modern Sexuality* (New York: Harper, 2010); Daniel Bergner, *What Do Women Want? Adventures in the Science of Female Desire* (New York: Ecco, 2013).

4. Andreas Baranowski and Heiko Hecht, "Gender Differences and Similarities in Receptivity to Sexual Invitations: Effects of Location and Risk Perception," *Archives of Sexual Behaviour* 44, no. 8 (April 2015).

5. Russell Clark and Elaine Hatfield, "Gender Differences in Receptivity to Sexual Offers," *Journal of Psychology and Human Sexuality* 2, no. 1 (1989): 39–55.

6. Margaret Atwood, "Writing the Male Character," in *Second Words: Selected Critical Prose* (Toronto: Anansi, 1982).

7. Meredith Chivers and Amanda Timmers, "Effects of Gender and Relationship Context in Audio Narratives on Genital and Subjective Sexual Response in Heterosexual Women and Men," *Archives of Sexual Behaviour* 41, no. 1 (March 2012): 185–197.

8. The English version used here is Friedrich Engels, *The Origins of Family, Private Property, and the State*, trans. Ernest Untermann (Chicago: Charles H. Kerr & Co., 1902), available online at Archive.org, http://www.archive.org/stream/theoriginofthefa33111gut/33111-8.txt.

9. See Elizabeth Brake, *Minimizing Marriage: Marriage, Morality, and the Law* (New York: Oxford University Press, 2012).

10. "Project Vox" is a contemporary research enterprise that "seeks to recover the lost voices of women who have been ignored in standard

narratives of the history of modern philosophy," aiming "to change those narratives, thereby changing what students around the world learn about philosophy's history." It can be explored at "Project Vox," Duke University Libraries, http://projectvox.library.duke.edu/pg.

11. Simon May, *Love: A History* (New Haven, CT: Yale University Press, 2011).

12. A group of psychologists and philosophers (Meredith Meyer, Andrei Cimpian, and Sarah-Jane Leslie) recently conducted empirical studies to explore the hypothesis that "women are likely to be under-represented in fields thought to require raw intellectual talent—a sort of talent that women are stereotyped to possess less of than men." They found evidence that "the academic fields believed by laypeople to re-quire brilliance are also the fields with lower female representation." See Meredith Meyer, Andrei Cimpian, and Sarah-Jane Leslie, "Women Are Underrepresented in Fields Where Success Is Believed to Require Brilliance," *Frontiers of Psychology* (March 11, 2015). The paper can be read online at http://www.princeton.edu/~sjleslie/Frontiers2015.pdf.

13. The version cited is Friedrich Nietzsche, *The Joyful Wisdom*, trans. Thomas Common (New York: Macmillan, 1910), available online at Archive.org, https://archive.org/stream/completenietasch10nietuoft /completenietasch10nietuoft_djvu.txt. Nietzsche's original German text was first published in 1882. The word "gay" that appears in the stan-dard English translation of this book's title (used in the main text) has nothing to do with queerness. It means (approximately) "happy," and the phrase "the gay science" refers to the technical skill or craft elements involved in writing poetry.

14. Friedrich Nietzsche, *Beyond Good and Evil: Prelude to a Phi-losophy of the Future*, trans. Helen Zimmern (New York: Macmillan, 1907), available online at Project Gutenberg, http://www.gutenberg .org/files/4363/4363-h/4363-h.htm. The original German text was first published in 1886.

15. Friedrich Nietzsche, *Ecce Homo: How One Becomes What One Is*, trans. Anthony M. Ludovici (New York: Macmillan, 1911), available online at Archive.org, https://archive.org/details/TheCompleteWorks OfFriedrichNietz-schevol.17-EcceHomo. The original German text was first published in 1908.

16. The version cited here is Arthur Schopenhauer, *The World as Will and Idea*, trans. R. B. Haldane and J. Kemp (London: Kegan Paul, Trench, Trübner & Co., 1909), available online at Project Gutenberg,

http://www.gutenberg.org/files/40868/40868-h/40868-h.html. Schopenhauer's original German text was published in 1818, and it is now commonly known as *The World as Will and Representation*.

17. For more on this idea, which has its roots in feminist standpoint theory, see section 2.1 of Heidi Grasswick, "Feminist Social Epistemology," *Stanford Encyclopedia of Philosophy*, 2013, http://plato.stanford.edu /entries/feminist-social-epistemology.

18. Simone de Beauvoir, *The Second Sex*, trans. Constance Borde and Sheila Malovany-Chevalier (New York: Alfred A. Knopf, 2009). The original French text was published in 1949.

19. An excellent resource here is Sally Haslanger's *Resisting Reality: Social Construction and Social Critique* (New York: Oxford University Press, 2012).

20. Berit Brogaard, *On Romantic Love: Simple Truths About a Complex Emotion* (New York: Oxford University Press, 2015).

Notes to Chapter 4

1. This hypothesis is popular; it comes up often in conversations with audiences when I present work on the nature of love.

2. This is my sense of the theory presented in Thomas Lewis, Fari Amini, and Richard Lannon's *A General Theory of Love* (New York: Vintage Books, 2000). Lewis and his coauthors are not very clear about their metaphysics of love. (This is not a criticism. Their goals differ from mine: they are psychiatrists, motivated by clinical effectiveness.) However, it seems to me that while they claim that art and poetry are sources of insight concerning love, their theory is ultimately neurobiological.

3. In *About Love: Reinventing Romance for Our Times* (Lanham, MD: Rowman & Littlefield, 1994), philosopher Robert Solomon takes this position. Solomon calls romantic love "one of the great ongoing innovations of Western culture," saying that although it "may begin" in biology, it is ultimately "a social invention."

4. One example of this occurs in Julian Savulescu and Anders Sandberg, "Neuroenhancement of Love and Marriage: The Chemicals Between Us," *Neuroethics* 1, no. 1 (March 2008): 31–44. The authors say, "The evolutionary systems form a ground on top of which the cultural and individual variants of love are built." But they do not explain this "grounding" metaphor except by mentioning cultural differences in "expression" (which returns us to the first strategy on the list).

5. The strategy I'm going to try is inspired by a tradition in twentieth- and twenty-first-century metaphysics, associated with Australian philosophers David Lewis and Frank Jackson, known as "The Canberra Plan." For an accessible introduction to some of this background, I recommend Daniel Nolan, *David Lewis* (Montreal: McGill-Queen's University Press, 2005), esp. chap. 9 ("Some Reflections on Lewis's Method").

6. Sue Johnson, *Love Sense: The Revolutionary New Science of Romantic Relationships* (Boston: Little, Brown & Co., 2013).

7. This is highlighted in Niko Bell, "Love Sense Author Says We're (Mostly) Like Monogamous Voles," *Xtra Vancouver*, January 26, 2014, http://dailyxtra.com/vancouver/news-and-ideas/newestlove-sense-author-says-we're-mostly-like-monogamous-voles-78045.

8. Helen Fisher, *Why We Love: The Nature and Chemistry of Romantic Love* (New York: Henry Holt & Co., 2004).

9. Timothy Taylor, *The Artificial Ape: How Technology Changed the Course of Human Evolution* (New York: Palgrave Macmillan, 2010). A summary of some of the core ideas can be found in David Keys, "Prehistoric Baby Sling 'Made Our Brains Bigger,'" *Independent*, September 6, 2010, http://www.independent.co.uk/life-style/history/prehistoric-baby-sling-made-our-brains-bigger-2071291.html.

10. Christopher Ryan and Cacilda Jethá discuss such models in chapters 6 and 7 of *Sex at Dawn: The Prehistoric Origins of Modern Sexuality* (New York: Harper, 2010).

11. See K. E. Starkweather and R. Hames, "A Survey of Non-Classical Polyandry," *Human Nature* 23, no. 2 (2012): 149–172.

12. Christopher Ryan and Cacilda Jethá, *Sex at Dawn: The Prehistoric Origins of Modern Sexuality* (New York: Harper, 2010).

13. Rafael Wlodarski, John Manning, and R. I. M. Dunbar, "Stay or Stray? Evidence for Alternative Mating Strategy Phenotypes in Both Men and Women," *Biology Letters* 11, no. 2 (February 2015).

14. Dietrich Klusmann, "Sexual Motivation and the Duration of Partnership," *Archives of Sexual Behaviour* 31, no. 3 (June 2002): 275–287.

15. Meredith L. Chivers and Amanda D. Timmers, "Effects of Gender and Relationship Context in Audio Narratives on Genital and Subjective Sexual Response in Heterosexual Women and Men," *Archives of Sexual Behaviour* 41, no. 1 (February 2012): 185–197.

16. Helen Fisher, *Why We Love: The Nature and Chemistry of Romantic Love* (New York: Henry Holt & Co., 2004).

17. Television has given Kilgrave the impression that he is entitled to a woman if he wants her and that abusive behaviors like stalking will eventually win her heart (as in romantic comedies). In chapter 6, I'll say more about the damaging gender norms built into society's image of romantic love.

18. Eva Illouz's *Why Love Hurts: A Sociological Explanation* (Cambridge, UK: Polity Press, 2012) is a fascinating exploration of the significance of choice in modern romantic love and how it interacts with economic considerations and gender roles. Illouz challenges the view of romantic love as an individualistic phenomenon, highlighting the extent to which it is shaped by institutional and cultural forces on a larger scale.

19. Elizabeth Brake's *Minimizing Marriage: Marriage, Morality, and the Law* (New York: Oxford University Press, 2012) explores this phenomenon in depth.

20. Berit Brogaard, *On Romantic Love: Simple Truths About a Complex Emotion* (New York: Oxford University Press, 2015).

Notes to Chapter 5

1. If you work in a coffee shop and run this last experiment with your tip jars, I would love to hear the results.

2. For overviews of some recent work on this kind of phenomenon, see Jonathan Haidt, *The Righteous Mind: Why Good People Are Divided by Politics and Religion* (New York: Pantheon Books, 2012), or Cordelia Fine, "The Pigheaded Brain," in *A Mind of Its Own: How Your Brain Distorts and Deceives* (New York: W. W. Norton & Co., 2006).

3. In contemporary studies, people in love with same-sex partners are found to be exhibiting just the same brain activity as opposite-sex partners when viewing images of loved ones. A study by neurobiologists Semir Zeki and John Paul Romayna found that when subjects viewed loved partners, "the pattern of activation and de-activation was very similar in the brains of males and females, and heterosexuals and homosexuals. We could therefore detect no difference in activation patterns between these groups." See Semir Zeki and John Paul Romayna, "The Brain Reaction to Viewing Faces of Opposite- and Same-Sex Romantic Partners," *PLoS ONE* 5, no. 12 (2006).

4. Lord Holt in *R v. Mawgridge*, 1707. Sue Bandalli discusses this case and this wording in "Provocation: A Cautionary Note," *Journal*

of Law and Society 22, no. 3 (September 1995): 398–409. Bandalli argues that provocation is unlikely to work as a defense for a woman since "ultimately the success or failure of a provocation defence depends on ingrained cultural judgment, and the hidden agenda of this partial defence, as it operates in practice in spousal homicide, is one of female responsibility, whether as victim or offender."

5. Harriet Harman, UK women's minister at the time of the change, is quoted on this point in Simon Maybin, "Are Murder Laws Sexist?," BBC, October 15, 2014, http://www.bbc.com/news /magazine-29612916.

6. The law and its previous versions can be accessed at "Criminal Code (R.S.C., 1985, c. C-46)," Justice Laws website, http://laws-lois .justice.gc.ca/eng/acts/C 46/section-232 html.

7. This code is not itself law, but its provisions have been adopted (in part or in whole) by many individual states.

8. Details of these cases and others can be found in Victoria Nourse, "Passion's Progress: Modern Law Reform and the Provocation Defense," *Yale Law Journal* 106, no. 5 (March 1997): 1331–1448.

9. The guidelines can be found on the US Sentencing Commission website, "2015 Chapter 5," http://www.ussc.gov/guidelines -manual/2015/2015-chapter-5.

10. In a 2014 article on the "gay panic" defense. See Justin Ling, "Why Do Canadian Courts Still Allow the 'Gay Panic' Defence?," *Daily Xtra*, February 8, 2014, http://www.dailyxtra.com/canada/news-and -ideas/news/canadian-courts-still-allow-the-gay-panic%E2%80%99 -defence-78795.

11. The wording can be found on the California Legislative Information website, "AB-2501 Voluntary Manslaughter (2013–2014)," https://leginfo.legislature.ca.gov/faces/billNavClient.xhtml?bill _id=201320140AB2501.

12. You can find information about how nonconscious (or "implicit") associations work at "Project Implicit," Harvard University, https://implicit.harvard.edu/implicit/faqs.html.

13. These statistics are from the FBI, accessible at "Crime in the United States 2013," FBI, https://www.fbi.gov/about-us/cjis /ucr/crime-in-the-u.s/2013/crime-in-the-u.s.-2013/offenses -known-to-law-enforcement/expanded-homicide/expanded_homicide _data_table_10_murder_circumstances_by_relationship_2013.xls, and https://www.fbi.gov/about-us/cjis/ucr/crime-in-the-u.s/2013

/crime-in-the-u.s.-2013/offenses-known-to-law-enforcement/expanded
-homicide. (The categories for "wife" and "husband" include common
-law spouses and ex-spouses.)

14. As reported in the full text of the case in the Supreme Court,
available at "Loving v. Virginia, 388 U. S. 1 (1967)," Nolo, http://supreme
.nolo.com/us/388/1/case.html.

15. See Frank Newport, "In U.S., 87% Approve of Black-White
Marriage, vs. 4% in 1958," Gallup, July 25, 2013, http://www.gallup.com
/poll/163697/approve-marriage-blacks-whites.aspx.

16. Maria Root, *Love's Revolution: Interracial Marriage* (Philadelphia: Temple University Press, 2001).

Notes to Chapter 6

1. Lisa Grunwald and Stephen Adler, *The Marriage Book: Centuries
of Advice, Inspiration, and Cautionary Tales from Adam and Eve to Zoloft*
(New York: Simon and Schuster, 2015).

2. Some representative statistics from the United States can be
found in summaries of the American Time Use Surveys published by
the Bureau of Labor Statistics. Recent figures are available at "American
Time Use Survey Summary," Bureau of Labor Statistics, June 24, 2015,
http://www.bls.gov/news.release/atus.nr0.htm.

3. Marianne Bertrand, Emir Kamenica, and Jessica Pan, "Gender
Identity and Relative Income Within Households," *Quarterly Journal of
Economics* 130, no. 2 (2015): 571–614. These data are for hetero married
couples in the United States in which both husband and wife earn positive income and are aged eighteen to sixty-five.

4. Marianne Bertrand et al. report, "The distribution of the share
of income earned by the wife exhibits a sharp drop to the right of 1/2,
where the wife's income exceeds the husband's income."

5. A summary of the current situation can be found at Sara Ashley
O'Brien, "78 Cents on the Dollar: The Facts About the Gender Wage
Gap," *CNN Money*, April 14, 2015, http://money.cnn.com/2015/04/13
/news/economy/equal-pay-day-2015.

6. Bertrand and her coauthors borrow this phrase from the title of
Arlie Russell Hochschild and Anne Machung's *The Second Shift: Working Parents and the Revolution at Home* (New York: Viking, 1989).

7. Laurie Rudman and Jessica Heppen, "Implicit Romantic Fantasies and Women's Interest in Personal Power," *Personality and Social
Psychology Bulletin* 29, no. 11 (November 2003): 1357–1370.

8. The same metaphor is developed extensively in Susan Weisser, *The Glass Slipper: Women and Love Stories* (New Brunswick, NJ: Rutgers University Press, 2013). This book critiques the social "script" for romantic love from a feminist perspective by means of a thorough examination of love stories.

9. Simone de Beauvoir, *The Second Sex*, trans. Constance Borde and Sheila Malovany-Chevalier (New York: Alfred A. Knopf, 2009).

10. Shulamith Firestone, *The Dialectic of Sex: The Case for Feminist Revolution* (New York: William Morrow, 1970.)

11. Terri Conley et al., "The Fewer the Merrier? Assessing Stigma Surrounding Consensually Non-monogamous Romantic Relationships," *Analyses of Social Issues and Public Policy* 13, no. 1 (December 2013): 1–30.

12. Kat Stoeffel, "Meet Terri Conley: The Psychologist with an Alternative Theory of Hookup Culture," *New York Times Magazine*, February 4, 2014, http://nymag.com/thecut/2014/02/woman-with-an-alternative-theory-of-hookups.html.

13. If my boyfriend had been gay, that could have been tolerated because, as his father pointed out to him, "even Obama says gays are OK" these days.

14. There was a conviction for adultery in Virginia in 2004. The penalty was community service. An interesting discussion of this case appeared the same year: Jonathan Turley, "Of Lust and the Law," *Washington Post*, September 5, 2004, http://www.washingtonpost.com/wp-dyn/articles/A62581-2004Sep4.html. The article points out that this was an opportunity to overturn an outdated law, but because the accused eventually accepted punishment, this was not possible.

15. This particular phrasing comes from the testimony of a poly gay man in a three-person relationship: Victor M. Feraru, "Will Polygamy Have Its Day in the Sun?," *HuffPost Queer Voices* (blog), July 23, 2013, http://www.huffingtonpost.com/victor-lopez/will-polygamy-have-its-day-in-the-sun_b_3629785.html.

16. Jonathan Frakes, dir., *Star Trek: First Contact* (Los Angeles, CA: Paramount Pictures, 1996).

17. Eli Lehrer, "Gay Marriage Good, Polyamory Bad," *HuffPost Politics*, January 23, 2014, http://www.huffingtonpost.com/eli-lehrer/gay-marriage-good-polyamo_b_4165423.html.

18. Some analysis of longitudinal data on class and educational similarities among spouses can be found in Monika Krzyżanowska and C. G. Nicholas Mascie-Taylor, "Educational and Social Class Assortative

Mating in Fertile British Couples," *Annals of Human Biology* 41, no. 6 (2014): 561–567. Over 60 percent of the couples they studied had identical levels of education.

19. In the early chapters of *Why Love Hurts: A Sociological Explanation* (Cambridge, UK: Polity Press, 2012), sociologist Eva Illouz discusses how certain formal restrictions on marrying outside one's social class were dissolved during the twentieth century and how that impacted women's and men's experiences of romantic love.

20. See Elizabeth Armstrong et al., "'Good Girls': Gender, Social Class, and Slut Discourse on Campus," *Social Psychology Quarterly* 77, no. 2 (June 2014): 100–122.

21. It's not lost on me that I am privileged to be able to talk about my polyamory in this book without immediate fear of losing my job, my home, or my family. Bertrand Russell appears to express something similar—though at a rather more advanced level—in a wry footnote in *Marriage and Morals* (New York: Liveright, 1929). In the main text he has been explaining that a professional man would lose his job for living in "open sin," but the footnote adds, "Unless he happens to teach at one of the older universities and to be closely related to a peer who has been a Cabinet minister."

22. The word "spinster" has undergone some recent attempts at reclamation, with limited success. See, for example, Kate Bolick's *Spinster: Making a Life of One's Own* (New York: Crown Publishers, 2015).

23. See Michel Reynaud et al., "Is Love Passion an Addictive Disorder?," *American Journal of Drug and Alcohol Abuse* 36, no. 5 (September 2010): 261–267.

24. Bertrand Russell, *Marriage and Morals* (New York: Liveright, 1929).

25. Marina Adshade, "Actually, Men Have Always Wanted Children More Than Women Have," *Globe and Mail*, March 30, 2015, http://www.theglobeandmail.com/globe-debate/actually-men -have-always-wanted-children-more-than-women/article23681771.

26. This is a point that Christopher Ryan and Cacilda Jethá emphasize in *Sex at Dawn: The Prehistoric Origins of Modern Sexuality* (New York: Harper, 2010).

Notes to Chapter 7

1. Thomas Lewis, Fari Amini, and Richard Lannon, *A General Theory of Love* (New York: Vintage Books, 2000).

2. Paul MacLean developed the idea of a "limbic system" in the 1940s and 1950s. It has proved controversial; Joseph LeDoux provides a summary of objections to it in *The Emotional Brain* (New York: Simon and Schuster, 1996).

3. See Christopher Faraone, *Ancient Greek Love Magic* (Cambridge, MA: Harvard University Press, 1999), for a tour of some of this history.

4. See Lawrence Babb, "The Physiological Conception of Love in the Elizabethan and Early Stuart Drama," *Publications of the Modern Language Association of America* 56, no. 4 (December 1941).

5. Today we have only fragments of Sappho's work; this one is known as fragment 31.

6. This wording comes from *Plato in Twelve Volumes*, Vol. 9, trans. Harold N. Fowler (Cambridge, MA: Harvard University Press, 1925), available through Perseus Digital Library, Tufts University, http://www.perseus.tufts.edu/hopper/text?doc=Perseus%3Atext %3A1999.01.0174%3Atext%3DPhaedrus%3Asection%3D245c.

7. Here I again draw upon Babb's "The Physiological Conception of Love in the Elizabethan and Early Stuart Drama."

8. André du Laurens, *Discourse of the Preservation of the Sight, of Melancholike Diseases, of Rheumes, and of Old Age*, translation of 1599 by Richard Surphlet (London: Shakespeare Association Facsimiles, 1938).

9. Ovid, *Remedia Amoris*, in *The Art of Love and Other Poems*, trans. J. H. Mozley; rev. G. P. Goold (Cambridge, MA: Harvard University Press, 1979), available through the digital Loeb Classical Library, http://www .loebclassics.com/view/ovid-remedies_love/1929/pb_LCL232.177.xml.

10. Joseph Frascella et al., "Shared Brain Vulnerabilities Open the Way for Non-substance Addictions: Carving Addiction at a New Joint?," *Annals of the New York Academy of Sciences* 1187 (February 2010): 294–315.

11. Brian Earp et al., "Addicted to Love: What Is Love Addiction and When Should It Be Treated?," *Philosophy, Psychiatry and Psychology* (2015). See also Brian Earp et al., "If I Could Just Stop Loving You: Anti-love Biotechnology and the Ethics of a Chemical Breakup," *American Journal of Bioethics* 13, no. 11 (2013): 3–17.

12. See Julian Savulescu and Anders Sandberg, "Neuroenhancement of Love and Marriage: The Chemicals Between Us," *Neuroethics* 1, no. 1 (March 2008): 31–44.

13. See Fiona Macdonald, "Scientists Can Now Tell If You're in Love by Scanning Your Brain," *Science Alert*, March 16, 2015,

http://www.sciencealert.com/scientists-can-now-tell-if-you-re-in-love
-by-scanning-your-brain.

14. Hongwen Song et al., "Love-Related Changes in the Brain: A
Resting-State Functional Magnetic Resonance Imaging Study," *Frontiers of Human Neuroscience* (February 13, 2015), http://www.ncbi.nlm
.nih.gov/pubmed/25762915.

15. Among other issues, the questionnaire assumes that passionate love is monogamous. I discuss this and other methodological problems for studies of romantic love in Carrie Jenkins, "Knowing Our Own
Hearts: Self-Reporting and the Science of Love," forthcoming in *Philosophical Issues*.

Notes to Coda

1. At the biological level, love can even share overlapping brain circuitry with sexual desire. See, for example, Stephanie Cacioppo et al.,
"The Common Neural Bases Between Sexual Desire and Love: A Mul-
tilevel Kernel Density fMRI Analysis," *Journal of Sexual Medicine* 9, no.
4 (April 2012): 947–1232.

2. See "Esther Perel: The Secret to Desire in a Long-Term Relationship," TED, February 2013, https://www.ted.com/talks/esther
_perel_the_secret_to_desire_in_a_long_term_relationship.

3. Brian D. Earp, Anders Sandberg, and Julian Savulescu, "Natu-
ral Selection, Childrearing, and the Ethics of Marriage (and Divorce):
Building a Case for the Neuroenhancement of Human Relationships,"
Philosophy and Technology 25, no. 4 (December 2012): 561–587.

4. See Frank Newport, "In U.S., 87% Approve of Black-White
Marriage, vs. 4% in 1958," Gallup, July 25, 2013, http://www.gallup
.com/poll/163697/approve-marriage-blacks-whites.aspx.

5. Such traditionalism is often explicitly premised on ideas about
what Christianity requires in marriage. See, for example, Stephanie
Samuel, "Should Couples Personalize Their Marriage Vows? Russell Moore Says No," *Christian Post*, November 13, 2014, http://www
.christianpost.com/news/russell-moore-on-personalize-vows-marriage
-is-about-accountability-to-the-entire-body-of-christ-129606.

6. See Daniel Nolan, "Temporary Marriage," in *After Marriage: Re-
thinking Marital Relationships*, ed. Elizabeth Brake (New York: Oxford
University Press, 2016).

7. This wording is from a message sent to me by a stranger.

8. In an episode of *Star Trek: The Next Generation* titled "The Outcast" (Robert Scheerer, dir., air date March 14, 1992), a structurally similar possibility is envisaged: an alien society engaging in the cultural and medical suppression of gender.

Index

A10 cells, 31
abuse, 6, 8, 127, 158–159, 162
actor analogy, 82–84, 101, 108,
    170
Adam and Eve story, 97
"Addicted to Love" (song), 157
addiction, 31, 32, 141, 157–158
Adler, Stephen, 124
Adshade, Marina, 143–144
adultery, 71, 112, 134, 171–172,
    176
agape, 41
alien society analogy, 107–108
All About Love (hooks), 6
amatonormativity, 65, 103, 141,
    142, 145, 180
Amini, Fari, 147
analytic metaphysics, 11–12
analytic philosophy, 12, 68, 76
Anatomy of Melancholy (Burton),
    154
antimiscegenation laws, 117, 173
Aristophanes myth, 4–5
The Artificial Ape (Taylor), 90
As You Like It (Shakespeare), 152
attachment
    abusive, 159
    as romantic love, 22

association with oxytocin and
    vasopressin, 22, 23, 86
evolutionary explanation for,
    24, 87, 88
root of in "limbic system," 148
Atwood, Margaret, 62

Babb, Lawrence, 154
baby slings, 90
Baranowski, Andreas, 61–62
Beall, Anne, 42–45, 75, 109, 119
Beauvoir, Simone de, 73–74,
    129–130
behavioral/therapeutic
    interventions, 155–156
Bergner, Daniel, 61
Bertrand, Marianne, 127, 128
Beyoncé, 126, 153
Beyond Good and Evil (Nietzsche),
    69
Bierce, Ambrose, 37
binaries, 105–106
biological determinism, 111–116,
    149
biological markers, 42
biology of love
    addiction, 31–32, 141,
    157–158

biology of love *(continued)*
  behavioral/therapeutic
    interventions, 155–156
  biological/medical
    interventions, 27–28,
    149–151, 154, 169
  evolution, 24, 87–90, 100,
    116–117
  false attributions to biology,
    85–86, 94–95, 99
  four humors theory, 20
  hormones, 21–23, 25, 27, 28
  importance for philosophy, 89
  love as neurochemical
    cocktail, 29, 100
  lust, evolutionary explanation
    for, 24
  methodology, questions
    about, 32–33, 96–97
  philosophical concerns about,
    33–35
  same-sex love, 110–111, 116
  as sexual desire, 20
  social bonding and
    cooperation, 91
  symptoms of, 152, 156–157,
    177–178
  universality of, 46–47, 83,
    141–142
  See also brain; Fisher
biology-society dilemma, 2–3, 47,
    80–81
bipedalism, 24, 88–90
brain
  A10 cells, 31
  activity, 29–31
  caudate nucleus, 21
  cortisol, 21, 27

dopamine, 21, 22, 25, 27, 28,
    42
fMRI (functional magnetic
    resonance imaging), 21,
    25, 164
oxytocin, 22, 23, 28, 42, 86,
    100, 178
testosterone, 22, 28
variability of love chemistry,
    29, 30
vasopressin, 22, 23, 28
ventral tegmental area, 21, 157
"The Brain in Love" (Fisher's
    TED talk), 31
Brake, Elizabeth, 65
Brogaard, Berit, 75, 102
Brown, Lucy, 157
Buffy the Vampire Slayer (TV
    show), 150
Burton, Robert, 154

Canada
  data on preferred number of
    children, 143–144
  implications of falling in love
    in, 43
  provocation, as legal defense,
    113
casual sex, 61–62
caudate nucleus, 21
change
  in acceptance of same-sex
    love, 140–141
  of cultural norms, 53–54, 85,
    99, 109–110, 113, 131
  future, 173–182
  influence of biology on, 27,
    34, 121

change *(continued)*
in interracial love, 173
in love and marriage, 40–41
as normal process, 120
in romantic love, 148–149
slowness of, xiv, 115, 168–169
to social role of love, 119–
121, 177
chemical breakup drugs, 28
chemical castration, 159
child rearing, 88, 91–92, 96, 175
"The Children of the Dirt"
(Rich), 5
Chinese culture and romantic
love, 45
Chivers, Meredith, 62, 95
Christianity, role of in oppression
of women, 60
composite image of love
amatonormativity, 142
changing, 144–146
customizing, 180–181
literature, 151–153
monogamy, 174–176
patterns, 129
popular representations of
love, 97–99, 131
presence of "normal" features,
102, 132
Conley, Terri, 133–134
conversion therapy, 159
cortisol, 21, 27
"Crazy In Love" (song), 153
"A Cross-Cultural Perspective
on Romantic Love"
(Jankoviak and Fischer),
46

daiquiri analogy, 29–30
definite descriptions, theory of, 56
The Dialectic of Sex (Firestone),
130
Diotima, 75
disability, love as, 156–157
Donne, John, 79
dopamine, 21, 22, 25, 27, 28, 42,
100, 177
drugs, use of, 158–163, 169–170
dual-nature theory, 12–14, 80–83,
108, 110–111, 116, 164,
179–180
Dunbar, Robin, 93

Earp, Brian, 171–172
Ecce Homo (Nietzsche), 70
Engels, Friedrich, 63–64
Enlightenment, social construct
of love during, 44, 48,
75–76
epigenetic effects, 28
equitable distribution argument,
160–161, 172
eros, 4, 41, 153
evolution, 24, 87–90, 100,
116–117
experiences, influence of, ix, 26,
64
extramarital sex, 64, 172

Facebook, 125
faithfulness, 39, 71–72, 112
female sexual dysfunction drug,
169–170
feminine mystique, 7, 69
feminism, 8, 70, 85, 129–130
financial inequality analogy, 137

Firestone, Shulamith, 129–130
Fischer, Edward, 46–47
Fisher, Helen, biological theory
    of love
  attachment as separate from
    romantic love, 23
  brain region and chemical
    involvement, 21–23, 25,
    100
  evolution, 24, 87–90, 100,
    116–117
  individual variations, 29
  Jenkins's analysis of, 23–26,
    32–35, 87–90, 95–97,
    100–101
  love as basic human drive,
    21–22, 25
  as standard model approach,
    91–92, 95–97
  "The Brain in Love" (TED
    talk), 31
Flibanserin, 169–170
fMRI (functional magnetic
    resonance imaging), 21,
    25, 164
Ford, Henry, 145
Foreigner, 4
four humors theory, 20, 150–151
free love, 57, 168
Friedan, Betty, 7, 69
future, predictions for
  customizing relationships,
    180–182
  dual nature of love, 179–180
  monogamy, 174–176
  polyamory, 179
  romantic love, 176–178

garage sale analogy, 77
The Gay Science (Nietzsche), 69
gay/trans panic, 114
gender assignment, 41–42
gender pay gap, 128
gender roles, 41, 87, 91, 94, 112,
    128–131
A General Theory of Love (Lewis,
    Amini, and Lannon), 148
Gilbert, W. S., 152
glass slipper effect, 128–129
Globe and Mail, 49, 143–144
Google, 5–6
Greeks, ancient
  four humors theory, 150–151
  kinds of love, 41
  love poetry, 151–152
  philosophical theories of love,
    4–5, 75
  marriage customs, 40
Grunwald, Lisa, 124

Haddaway, 4
*Harry Potter and the Half-Blood
    Prince* (Rowling), 150
hate crimes, 114
Hecht, Heiko, 61–62
Heppen, Jessica, 128
Her (film), xii, 33
heteronormativity, 66, 72, 110,
    130, 131, 132
Hippocrates, 150
historic views of love
  ancient Greece, 4–5, 41, 75,
    150–152
  Renaissance, 20, 154–155
  Romantic era, 44, 48
  Victorian era, 43–44

Hollywood, nonmonogamy in, 134
homophobia, 20, 85, 114
homosexuality, 50, 57, 108. *See
also* queer love; same-sex
relationships
hooks, bell, 6, 8, 159
horse and carriage analogy,
123–124
HuffPost blog, on polyamory and
same-sex marriage, 135
hypothalamus, 23

"I Want to Know What Love Is"
(song), 4
ingroups and outgroups, 106
Internet, x, xii
interracial relationships, 117–118,
131, 139, 173
interventions, behavioral/
therapeutic, 154–156, 169
interventions, medical/biological,
27–28, 149–151, 154, 169

Jankoviak, Williams, 46–47
jealousy, 60, 112, 152, 171
Jenkins, Carrie, personal
experiences of, ix–xi, xiii,
38, 79–80, 102–103, 132,
134, 143
Jessica Jones (TV show), 97
Jethá, Cacilda, 19, 61, 92
Johnson, Sue, 86
Jonze, Spike, xii

K-I-S-S-I-N-G rhyme, 51, 60, 87,
97, 132
Kamenica, Emir, 127
Keats, John, 18

Kennedy, Anthony, 180
Kirkup, Kyle, 114
The Kiss (Klimt), 97
Klimt, Gustav, 97
Klusmann, Dietrich, 94

language,
social significance of, xi,
38–39, 113–114, 139,
141, 158–159, 161
theoretical significance of,
22, 76
Lannon, Richard, 147
Laurens, André du, 154
laws, 50
Lehrer, Eli, 135–136
L'elisir d'amour (Donizetti opera),
150
lesbians, 96, 108–109
Lewis, Thomas, 147
limbic system, 148
love. *See* romantic love
Love: A History (May), 67, 72
love-conquers-all narratives, 138
love-melancholy, 20, 154, 158
love potions, 150
Love Sense (Johnson), 86
*Love's Revolution: Interracial
Marriage* (Root), 118
Loving v. Virginia (1967), 117
lust
in ancient Greece, 41
association with testosterone,
22
chemically induced, 160
evolutionary explanation for,
24
in relationships, 94–95

madness, 152–153
magic
  kinds of, 149–151
  of love, 9, 14, 17, 19, 100
  in nature, 18
Manning, John, 93
marital rape, 169
marriage
  in ancient Greece, 40
  arranged, 48
  equality, 125–126
  faithfulness, 71–72, 72
  interracial, 117–118
  love-marriage connection,
    40–41, 51, 59–60, 98,
    123–127, 131
  morganatic, 138
  open, 60
  as property transaction, 40,
    124
  purpose, 59–60, 63
  romantic love and, 40–41
  same-sex, 109, 135
  temporary, 93, 174–175
  traditional, 124, 145
Marriage and Morals (Russell),
    56–59, 68–69, 172
The Marriage Book (Grunwald and
    Adler), 124
mass media, xii, xv
Match.com, 19
maternal instinct, 21
May, Simon, 67
medical/biological interventions,
    27–28, 149–151, 154, 169
medicalization of love, 151–154,
    156–158
medicine analogy, 18

melancholy, 151
men
  casual sex, 62
  desire for children, 143–144
  dangers of romantic love for,
    74
  dominance of philosophy by,
    68–69
  extramarital sex, 172
  faithfulness, 71
  gender roles, 112, 127
  men's rights activists, 70, 155
  monogamy and, 60, 63, 86
  Nietzsche's view of, 69
  patriarchal polygamy,
    135–136
  sex-related violence by,
    112–115
  stud as positive appellation,
    139
  See also patriarchy
metaphysics, 1–2, 11
The Mikado (Gilbert and
    Sullivan), 152
Mills, Charles, 74
monogamy
  Bertrand Russell on, 60–61,
    63
  child care and, 91–92
  evolutionary theory of, 24,
    87–88
  female neediness and, 88, 94
  future of, 174–176
  halo effect, 134
  in Hollywood, 134
  men and, 60, 63, 86
  as natural for humans, 63, 80,
    86–88

monogamy *(continued)*
  patriarchal, 92
  philosophers' treatment of,
    x–xi
  same-sex relationships and,
    133–135
  sex and, 60–61, 63, 71
  as social norm, 80, 133–135
  temporary, 93, 174–175
  women and, 63, 94–95
  See also nonmonogamy
Moore, G. E., 11
morganatic marriage, 138
"Mother's Little Helper" (song),
  170

natural behavior, perceptions of
  as biological phenomenon, 19,
    54, 79–80, 83, 120
  dominant ideology and,
    85–86, 89, 115, 117, 144
  monogamy, 63, 80, 86, 88
  social construct, 40–41
  toxic behaviors, justification
    for, 112
  for women, 69–74, 95
neurochemicals, 22
neuroscience, love and, 13
neurotransmitters, 21
Nietzsche, Friedrich, 69–72, 156
Nolan, Daniel, 174
nonmonogamy, xii–xv, 93, 102,
  133, 139, 140, 172
nontraditional love
  in mass media, xv
  polyamory, xii, 39, 133, 135,
    140, 175, 179
  polyandry, 92

polygamy, 91–92, 135
  safety issues, 134
  See also nonmonogamy;
    same-sex relationships
Nozick, Robert, 22–23, 30, 65
nuclear family
  children and, 140, 175
  as cooperative group, 91
  female neediness, 88–90, 94,
    116–117
  as tool of patriarchy, 130
  polyamory and, 140
  romantic love and, 41, 48,
    51–53, 60, 98–99, 101,
    118
  same-sex, 133, 140
  social norms and, 145

Obama, Barack, 125
objectivity, difficulties with,
  xv–xvi
OKCupid (website), x
On Romantic Love (Brogaard), 75,
  102
one-true-love-forever model,
  168–171, 174
*The Origins of the Family, Private
  Property and the State*
  (Engels), 63
online dating, 132
  Match.com, 19
  OKCupid, x
Outlaw, Lucius, 74
overthinking love, 9–10, 153, 181
Ovid, 70, 155, 156
oxytocin, 22, 23, 28, 42, 86, 100,
  178

pair-bonding, 24
Palmer, Robert, 157
Pan, Jessica, 127
patriarchal monogamy, 92
patriarchal polygamy, 91, 135–136
patriarchy, 60, 74, 129, 130
Perel, Esther, 169
Phaedrus (Plato), 153
phenotypes of mating strategy, 93
philia, 41
philosophers
    Beauvoir, Simone de 73–74, 129–130
    Brake, Elizabeth 65
    Brogaard, Berit 75, 102
    Earp, Brian 171–172
    Engels, Friedrich 63–64
    Firestone, Shulamith 129–130
    May, Simon 67
    Mills, Charles 74
    Nietzsche, Friedrich 69–72, 156
    Nolan, Daniel 174
    Nozick, Robert 22–23, 30, 65
    Outlaw, Lucius 74
    Plato, 1, 4–5, 59, 75,153
    Russell, Bertrand 56–61, 63–66, 68, 76
    Sandberg, Anders 171
    Savulescu, Julian 171
    Schopenhauer, Arthur 20, 71–72, 86
    Shand, John 9–10
    Socrates, 59, 75
    Turing, Alan, 50
    Wollstonecraft, Mary 74

philosophy
    nature of, 1–2, 12, 58–59, 77
    fallibility of, 77
    male dominance of, 67, 71
    privilege as hindrance, 72–73
Picard, Jean-Luc, 135
Plato, 1, 4–5, 59, 75, 153
politicization of love, 167–168
polyamory, xii, 39, 133, 135, 140, 175, 179
polyandry, 92
polygamy, 91–92, 135
popular culture, love in, 4
Porter, Cole, 4
prairie voles, 28, 86
premarital sex, 64
promiscuity, 38, 93, 139
provocation, as legal defense, 112–114
psychology, view of love, 3

Quarterly Journal of Economics, on household income data, 127
Queen, 153
queer love
    biology of, 110–111, 116
    as deviation from norm, 85
    homophobia, 85, 114
    romantic love, 115, 118, 119, 140, 159
    See also homosexuality; same-sex relationships
queer men, violence against, 114

race, used as impediment to love, 111, 118, 173
    social construction of, 49, 74
    and biology, 85, 100, 117

relationships
customizing, 180–181
interracial, 117–118, 131, 139,
173
nonmonogamous, xii–xv, 93,
102, 133, 139, 140, 172
polyamorous, xii, 39, 133,
135, 140, 175, 179
in popular culture, 4
See also monogamy; same-sex
religion
used as impediment to love,
111, 118
love-marriage connection, 97
oppression of women, 60
"Remedia Amoris" (Ovid), 155
Renaissance medicine, 20,
154–155
reproduction-love connection, 51,
53, 87–88, 95–99, 143,
145
Republic (Plato), 59
Reynaud, Michel, 141
Rich, Simon, 5
Rolling Stones, 170
Roman's eulogy for wife, 124–125
Romantic era, love in, 44, 48
romantic love
Beall-Sternberg theory,
42–45, 75, 109, 119
capacity for change, 103–104
"curing" love, 149, 151,
154–156, 158–159, 162,
164
dangers of, 74
dual-nature theory, 12–14,
80–83, 108, 110–111,
116, 164, 179–180
features of, 52

four humors theory, 20,
150–151
function of, 48, 51–53,
59–60, 98, 101, 118, 133,
137, 140, 142, 178
future of, 176–178
historic views of, 20, 43–44,
152–155
as "human universal" on
"biological core," 46
importance of understanding,
8, 10–11
inclusiveness, xiii–xiv, 103
interventions, 27–28, 149–
151, 154, 155–156, 169
Jankoviak-Fischer theory,
46–47
Lewis-Amini-Lannon theory,
147–148
love-marriage connection,
40–41, 51, 59–60, 98,
123–127, 131
love-reproduction connection,
51, 53, 87–88, 95–99,
143, 145
metaphysical questions about,
2
as mystery, 7–8
Nozick theory, 22–23, 30,
65
philosophers' view of, x–xi,
3
politicization of, 167–168
public demand for
information about, 18
rationality of, 44, 76
as recent phenomenon, 40
refusal to acknowledge,
118–119

romantic love *(continued)*
　romantic love-private property
　　connection, 112–113,
　　136, 161, 175, 176
　safety issues for
　　nontraditionalists, 134
　saying "I love you," 6
　science of, 17–19, 26–35
　society's regulation of, 119
　tenacity of, 176–177
　variations of, 102
　as women's concern, 8
　See also biology of love;
　　Fisher; Russell; same-
　　sex relationships; social
　　constructionism
romantic mystique, 7–9, 17–19,
　148, 165
Romeo and Juliet (Shakespeare), 97
Root, Maria, 118
Rossetti, Christina, 123
Rudman, Laurie, 128
Russell, Bertrand
　amatonormative attitude,
　　65–66
　on children's effect on
　　marriage, 175
　desire to "excite protest," 56
　as founder of analytic
　　philosophy, 11–12
　on gendered desire for
　　children, 143–144
　heteronormative attitude of,
　　66
　on jealousy, 172
　love, views on, 59–60, 65
　marriage, views on, 60
　messages to future
　　generations, 179

Nobel Prize for Literature, 56
　on oppression of women,
　　60–61
　perception of philosophy as
　　male activity, 68
　sex, views on, 56–57, 56–61
　sex-positive movement and,
　　56
　social class advantage, 57
　theory of definite
　　descriptions, 56
　on widely held opinions, 173
　on wisdom of loving, 76
　on women's sexuality, 169
Ryan, Christopher, 19, 61, 92

same-sex relationships
　Aristophanes myth, 5
　attempts to "cure," 159
　Fisher's explanation for,
　　95–96
　laws against, 50, 57
　monogamy and, 133–135
　refusal to acknowledge love,
　　118–119
　romantic love and, 108–109,
　　115, 130–131
　social acceptance of, 140–141
　social change, 110–111
　See also homosexuality; queer
　　love
Sandberg, Anders, 171
Sappho, 151–152
Savage, Dan, xii, 57, 60
Savulescu, Julian, 171
Schopenhauer, Arthur, 20, 71–72,
　86
Science Alert (website), 163
science of love, 17–19, 26–35

scientific method, advantages of, 27

The Second Sex (de Beauvoir), 73–74, 129

Serenity Prayer, 147, 165

sex

  casual, 61–62

  extramarital, 64

  monogamy and, 60–61, 63, 71

  premarital, 64

  promiscuity, 38, 93, 139

  Russell's view of, 56–57, 59

  Schopenhauer's view of, 71

  in Victorian culture, 44

Sex at Dawn (Ryan and Jethá), 19, 61, 92

sex-positive movement, 56, 64

sexual desire

  and women, 60–61, 94–95

  connection to romantic love, 43, 51, 53, 98, 169–170

  in Victorian era, 43

Shakespeare, William, 17, 55, 97, 105, 152, 153, 167

Shand, John, 9–10

Shatner, William aka Captain Kirk, 84

short-term promiscuous bonding, 93

slut, meaning of, 38

slut shaming, 138–139

slut-*versus*-stud phenomenon, 139

soccer game analogy, 120

social class

  and privilege, 57, 67, 72

  love and, 111, 118, 138

  relationship to gender and nonmonogamy, 137–139

"The Social Construction of Love" (Beall and Sternberg), 42

social constructionism

  changes to love's social role, 119–121, 177

  cultural representations, 97–99

  cultural variations, 44–45

  current norms, 99

  falling in love, 43

  familiarity, role of, 40

  function of romantic love, 48, 52–53, 59–60

  gender stereotypes, 41, 73, 125, 127–131, 145, 160, 173, 175

  influence of society, 37–38, 42, 45

  Jenkins's analysis of, 45–54

  localization of, 83

  need for change, 144–145

  reactions to author's lifestyle, 38

  reality of social constructs, 49

  as social force, 6–7

  traditional love as "normal," xiv–xv, 45, 51–52, 65

  variety of social structures, 52

  See also same-sex relationships

social stability, 137–140, 142, 168, 175

society-biology dilemma, 2–3, 13, 47, 79–81

socioeconomic status, 137

Socrates, 59, 75

Sonnet 147 (Shakespeare), 152

soul mates, 4, 5

stability, social, 137–140, 142, 168, 175
standard model approach, 95–97, 178
Star Trek (TV show), 84
Statistics Canada General Social Survey, 143–144
"Stay or Stray? Evidence for Alternative Mating Strategy Phenotypes in Both Men and Women" (Wlodarski, Manning, and Dunbar), 93
Sternberg, Robert, 42–45, 47–48, 75, 109, 119
stigma, xii, 62, 99, 126, 133–135
stud, 139
Symposium (Plato), 4, 59, 75

Taylor, Timothy, 90
temporary monogamy/marriage, 93, 174–175
testosterone, 22, 28
theories of love. *See* Beall; dual nature; Fisher; Jankoviak; Lewis; Nozick; Russell
Timmers, Amanda, 62, 95
traditional marriage, 124, 145
    See also nuclear family
Trinity College, Cambridge, 11
Turing, Alan, 50
Twitter, 125
union view of love, 65
United Kingdom (UK)
    love in Victorian England, 43–44
    male homosexuality, law against, 50

marital rape, 169
provocation, as legal defense, 112–114
same-sex marriage, 109
United States
    adultery laws, 134
    antimiscegenation laws, 117, 173
    California Penal Code, 114
    female murder victims, statistics on, 115
    household income data, 127–128
    marital rape, 169
    Model Penal Code, 113–114
    Sentencing Commission, 113–114
    Supreme Court, 117, 125–126, 141, 180

vasopressin, 22, 23, 28
ventral tegmental area, 21, 31, 157
Viagra, 169
violence, 114–115, 136, 159

Wente, Margaret, 49
Western nations, social construct of love in, 48
What Do Women Want? (Bergner), 61
"What Is Love?" (song), 4
"What Is This Thing Called Love?" (song), 4
When Harry Met Sally (film), 97
White, E. B., 18
White, K. S., 18
Why We Love: The Nature and Chemistry of Romantic Love (Fisher), 21, 95–96

Wikipedia, 3
wisdom, 76, 147, 148, 165
Wittgenstein, Ludwig, 11
Wlodarski, Rafael, 93
Wollstonecraft, Mary, 74
women
abuse of, 125
casual sex, 62, 125
dangers of romantic love, 74
desire for children, 143–144
earning power in US, 128
faithfulness in marriage,
71–72
gender stereotypes, 41, 73,
125, 127–131, 145, 160,
173, 175
glass slipper effect, 128–129
infertile, 70
monogamy and, 63, 94–95

Nietzsche's view of, 69–72
oppression of, 60–61, 89, 125,
130
philosophy, exclusion of
women's voices in, 68
prehistoric female neediness,
88–90, 94, 116–117
premarital sex for, 64
as property, 112–113, 136,
161, 176
sexuality of, 61, 94–95, 169
violence and romantic
relationships, 115
*The World as Will and
Representation*
(Schopenhauer), 71

"You're Nobody 'til Somebody
Loves You" (song), 141

Credit: Jonathan Jenkins Ichikawa

Carrie Jenkins is professor of philosophy at the University of British Columbia, Vancouver, a nationally elected Canada Research Chair, and the principal investigator on the collaborative research project "The Nature of Love," funded by the Social Sciences and Humanities Research Council of Canada. She lives in Vancouver and tweets @carriejenkins.